English / Arabic
Phrasebook

(ara)

عربي / إنجليزي العبارات

earabi / 'iinjlizi aleibarat

John C. Rigdon

English / Arabic Phrasebook

English / Arabic Phasebook

عربي / إنجليزي العبارات

earabi / 'iinjlizi aleibarat

1st Printing – MAY 2016 CS

Published by:
Eastern Digital Resources
31 Bramblewood Dr. SW
Cartersville, Ga 30120 USA
http://www.wordsrus.info
EMAIL: Sales@wordsrus.info
Tel. (678) 739-9177

Contents

Introduction

This phrase book contains a guide to English pronunciation and Grammar, a guide to Arabic pronunciation and Grammar, sample phrases and sentences arranged by topic and a dictionary of 700 of the most commonly used words and phrases.

For pronunciation and definitions of the words in this book, see our website at

http://www.wordsrus.info

General

This book is based on Modern Standard Arabic (MSA). Modern Standard Arabic is a standardized form of Arabic used in business, literature, education, politics, and the media throughout the Arabic-speaking world. It's really a modernized form of classical Arabic, and it is not the same language as the spoken varieties found from Morocco to Iraq, but it's a good form of Arabic to familiarize yourself with as a tourist, because it is used as a common language in Arab countries.

Other volumes in this series address the major dialects.

- Dialects of Egypt and Sudan

- Dialects of the Arabian Peninsula

- Dialects of Syria, Lebanon and Palestine

- Dialects of Iraq

- Dialects of Morocco, Algeria, Tunisia and western Libya

Pronunciation

MSA has three vowels, **a** as in t<u>a</u>co, **i** as in h<u>i</u>m, and **u** as in p<u>u</u>t. There are long varieties of these vowels as well: **aa**, like a long ah, **ii** as in s<u>ee</u>, and **uu** as in t<u>oo</u>n. There are two diphthongs, **aw** as in h<u>ou</u>se, and **ay** as in b<u>i</u>te or b<u>ai</u>t. Most Arabic consonants are very similar to English or other familiar European languages: **b, d, s, t, k, sh, th** as in this as well as **th** as in <u>th</u>ink, rolled **r, gh** as in the French <u>r</u>ue, **kh** as in German a<u>ch</u>. Then there are the really "Arabic sounding" consonants, which may take a bit of practice! The letter **xayn** (also transcribed sometimes as 3) is produced with a tight constriction in the throat, not unlike a gag. The letter **H** sounds as though you're blowing on glasses to clean them. **Q** is like **k**, but from further back in the throat. The "emphatic" consonants **D, T, DH**, and **S** are all produced with the tongue pulled down and back, giving the vowels around them a "deeper" quality.

Vocabulary

MSA has some borrowings from English and other languages, so you'll come across words like **tilifizyuun** (*television*) or **kumbyuutar** (*computer*). But you won't be able to rely on cognates very often, because Arabic and English are not closely related. One important feature of Arabic and other Semitic languages is that words are built around.

Grammar

Some aspects of Arabic grammar are very similar to languages you may already have studied. But since Arabic is not closely related to English or other European languages, some grammatical concepts may be new to you.

Arabic nouns have gender, either masculine or feminine. Arabic has no indefinite article, but it does have the definite article al. Adjectives agree with nouns for gender and number, but there are actually three numbers: singular, plural, and dual (two of something). Adjectives also agree with nouns for definiteness: **al-kitaab al-jadiid** (lit,. *the-book the-new*, '*the new book.*')

There are only two basic tenses in Arabic, past and present. The future is expressed with the present tense and the particle **sa** or **sawfa** in front of the verb. There are two other "moods," the subjunctive and the jussive, which have certain specialized uses. Arabic verbs have a rich conjugation, with a total of 13 forms in each tense/mood once you figure in dual and both masculing/feminine forms. The past conjugation involves suffixes or endings (**katab-uu**, *they wrote*), but the present tense involves both prefixes and suffixes (**ya-ktub-uuna**, *they write*).

A major feature of Arabic and other Semitic languages is the triconsontal root, that is, a root form consisting of three consonants. For example, **k-t-b** has the general meaning of writing, and those consonants appear in verb forms, nouns, and even adjectives, with prefixes, suffixes, or different vowels interspersed between the root consonants. Some examples are: **kitaab** (*book*), **kutub** (*books*), **kataba** (*he wrote*), **yaktub** (*he writes*), **maktab** (*office*), **kaatib** (*writer*), **kutubii** (*bookseller*), **mukaataba** (*correspondence*), **maktuub** (*written down, predestined*).

What is Spoken Arabic / the Arabic Dialects?

Spoken Arabic (also called "Colloquial Arabic", or simply "Arabic Dialects") differs from Modern Standard Arabic in the following:

1.The grammatical structure is simpler.

2.Some letters are pronounced differently, and pronunciation also differs between dialects.

3.Some words and expressions are more or less unique to their respective dialects.

4.Spoken Arabic only occurs in written form when a humorist or popular touch is desired.

5. The vocabulary and style are more casual. Slang words and expressions are used that don't have equivalents in Modern Standard Arabic.

How many Arabic dialects are there?

Spoken Arabic can be broadly categorized into the following, main dialect groups:

• North African Arabic (Morocco, Algeria, Tunisia and Libya),

• Hassaniya Arabic (Mauritania),

• Egyptian Arabic,

• Levantine Arabic (Lebanon, Syria, Jordan and Palestine),

• Iraqi Arabic,

• Gulf Arabic (Kuwait, Bahrain, Qatar, the U.A.E. and Oman).

• Hejazi Arabic (Western Saudi Arabia)

• Najdi Arabic (Central Saudi Arabia).

• Yemeni Arabic (Yemen & southwestern Saudi Arabia).

How big are the differences between the Arabic dialects?

• Differences between dialects of the Middle East (Egypt, the Levant, Iraq and the Gulf) are small enough to enable Arabs of different nationalities to understand one another fairly well.

• North African dialects are more unique in structure and vocabulary, and can be a real challenge to understand, even to Arabs of the Middle East.

• Within the main dialect groups, there are regional sub-dialects. Like in other parts of the world, there are differences between the city language and the provincial dialects.

• The most widely understood dialects are Egyptian and Levantine Arabic. The Egyptian media industry has traditionally played a dominant in the Arab world. A huge number of cinema productions, television dramas and comedies have since long familiarized Arab audiences with the Egyptian dialect.

•The satellite television channels have made it easier for other dialects to reach wider audiences. Popular showbiz programs often have Lebanese hosts. This has given the Lebanese dialect something of a fashion status.

•If your interest is not limited to one particular country, you should choose Modern Standard Arabic. Once you have basic knowledge of Modern Standard Arabic, learning a dialect becomes an easy task.

•Learning to read, write and speak Modern Standard Arabic, and later learning the basics of a dialect, is the best route to sound knowledge of Arabic.

•Educated Arabs, from the middle class and upwards, are quite comfortable conversing in Modern Standard Arabic. Since this form of Arabic serves as a lingua franca across the Arabic-speaking world, speaking with a Mauritanian or an Omani becomes equally easy.

•The choice of language generally depends on the educational level of the person you are addressing. For instance, ordering a shawarma in the street is best done in the local dialect, and so is grabbing a cab.

•If you are going to spend just a short time in an Arab country, you should try to learn the basics of that country's main dialect. This would help you manage the basic day-to-day routines, although it would not make you understand anything written.

•It should be noted that many Arabs have attitudes towards certain dialects. For example, although held in high esteem in Egypt, the Cairo dialect is often looked upon with amusement by non-Egyptian Arabs.

•Finally, if you know Moroccan or Algerian Arabic, you can't use it in the Middle East (east of Libya), since nobody would understand what you are saying.

A Guide to English Pronunciation

English is not a phonetic language. It has borrowed many words from other languages and words are often not pronounced as they seem.

The sounds of English and the International Phonetic Alphabet:

http://www.antimoon.com/how/pronunc-soundsipa.htm

An excellent resource with videos for learning to pronounce English words;

http://rachelsenglish.com/

The English Alphabet

English Alphabet with Pronunciation

A a	B b	C c	D d	E e
[eɪ]	[bi:]	[si:]	[di:]	[i:]

F f	G g	H h	I i	J j
[ef]	[dʒi:]	[eɪtʃ]	[aɪ]	[dʒeɪ]

K k	L l	M m	N n	O o
[keɪ]	[el]	[em]	[en]	[əʊ]

P p	Q q	R r	S s	T t
[pi:]	[kju:]	[a:]	[es]	[ti:]

U u	V v	W w
[ju:]	[vi:]	['dʌbəlju:]

X x	Y y	Z z
[eks]	[waɪ]	[zed/zi:]

English Vowels

A

E

I

O

U

Y

Nouns

Nouns answer the questions **"What is it?"** and **"Who is it?"** They give names to things, people, and places.

Examples

- dog
- bicycle
- Mary
- girl
- beauty
- France
- world

In general there is no distinction between masculine, feminine in English nouns. However, gender is sometimes shown by different forms or different words when referring to people or animals.

Examples

Masculine	Feminine	Gender neutral
man	woman	person
father	mother	parent
boy	girl	child
uncle	aunt	

Masculine	Feminine	Gender neutral
husband	wife	spouse
actor	actress	
prince	princess	
waiter	waitress	server
rooster	hen	chicken
stallion	mare	horse

Many nouns that refer to people's roles and jobs can be used for either a masculine or a feminine subject, like for example *cousin, teenager, teacher, doctor, student, friend, colleague*

Examples

- Mary is my friend. She is a doctor.
- Peter is my cousin. He is a doctor.
- Arthur is my friend. He is a student.
- Jane is my cousin. She is a student.

It is possible to make the distinction for these neutral words by adding the words *male* or *female*.

Examples

- Sam is a female doctor.

- No, he is not my boyfriend, he is just a male friend.
- I have three female cousins and two male cousins.

Infrequently, nouns describing things without a gender are referred to with a gendered pronoun to show familiarity. It is also correct to use the gender-neutral pronoun (it).

Examples

- I love my car. **She** (the car) is my greatest passion.
- France is popular with **her** (France's) neighbours at the moment.
- I travelled from England to New York on the Queen Elizabeth; **she** (the Queen Elizabeth) is a great ship.

Adjectives

Adjectives describe the aspects of nouns. When an adjective is describing a noun, we say it is "modifying" it. Adjectives can:

Describe feelings or qualities

Examples

- He is a **lonely** man.
- They are **honest**.

Give nationality or origin

Examples

- I heard a **French** song.
- This clock is **German**.
- Our house is **Victorian**.

Tell more about a thing's characteristics

Examples

- That is a **flashy** car.
- The knife is **sharp**.

Tell us about age

Examples

- He's a **young** man.
- My coat is **old**.

Tell us about size and measurement

Examples

- John is a **tall** man.
- This film is **long**.

Tell us about color

Examples

- Paul wore a **red** shirt.
- The sunset was **crimson**.

Tell us what something is made of

Examples

- The table is **wooden**.
- She wore a **cotton** dress.

Tell us about shape

Examples

- I sat at a **round** table.
- The envelope is **square**.

Express a judgment or a value

Examples

- That was a **fantastic** film.

- Grammar is **complicated**.

Determiners

Determiners are words placed in front of a noun to make it clear what the noun refers to. Use the pages in this section to help you use English determiners correctly.

Determiners in English

- Definite article : the
- Indefinite articles : a, an
- Demonstratives: this, that, these, those
- Pronouns and possessive determiners : my, your, his, her, its, our, their
- Quantifiers : a few, a little, much, many, a lot of, most, some, any, enough
- Numbers : one, ten, thirty
- Distributives : all, both, half, either, neither, each, every
- Difference words : other, another
- Pre-determiners : such, what, rather, quite

Verbs

Selecting the correct verb tense and conjugating verbs correctly is tricky in English. Click on the verb tense to read more about how to form this tense and how it is used, or select a time to see the full list of tenses and references on that time.

Present Tenses in English	Examples
Simple present tense	They **walk** home.
Present continuous tense	They **are walking** home.

Past Tenses in English	
Simple past tense	Peter **lived** in China in 1965.
Past continuous tense	I **was reading** when she arrived.

Perfect Tenses in English	
Present perfect tense	I **have lived** here since 1987.

Present Tenses in English	Examples
Present perfect continuous	I **have been living** here for years.
Past perfect	We **had been** to see her several times before she visited us.
Past perfect continuous	He **had been watching** her for some time when she turned and smiled.
Future perfect	We **will have arrived** in the States by the time you get this letter.
Future perfect continuous	By the end of your course, you **will have been studying** for five years.

Future Tenses in English	
Simple future tense	They **will go** to Italy next week.
Future continuous tense	I **will be travelling** by train.

Conditional Tenses
in English

Zero conditional	If ice **gets** hot it **melts**.
Type 1 conditional	If he **is** late I **will be** angry.
Type 2 conditional	If he **was** in Australia he **would be getting up** now.
Type 3 conditional	She **would have visited** me if she **had had** time.
Mixed conditional	I **would be playing** tennis if I **hadn't broken** my arm.

The -ing forms in English

Gerund	I like **swimming**.
Present participle	She goes **running** every morning.

Adverbs

Adverbs are a very broad collection of words that may describe how, where, or when an action took place. They may also express the viewpoint of the speaker about the action, the intensity of an adjective or another adverb, or several other functions. Use these pages about the grammar of adverbs in English to become more precise and more descriptive in your speaking and writing.

Adverbs modify, or tell us more about, other words. Usually adverbs modify verbs, telling us how, how often, when, or where something was done. The adverb is placed after the verb it modifies.

Examples

- The bus moved **slowly**.
- The bears ate **greedily**.
- The car drove **fast**.

Sometimes adverbs modify adjectives, making them stronger or weaker.

Examples

- You look **absolutely** fabulous!
- He is **slightly** overweight.
- You are **very** persistent.

Some types of adverbs can modify other adverbs, changing their degree or precision.

Examples

- She played the violin **extremely** well.
- You're speaking **too** quietly.
-

Adverbs of time

Adverbs of time tell us when an action happened, but also for how long, and how often.

Adverbs that tell us when

Adverbs that tell us when are usually placed at the end of the sentence.

Examples

- Goldilocks went to the Bears' house **yesterday**.
- I'm going to tidy my room **tomorrow**.
- I saw Sally **today**.
- I will call you **later**.
- I have to leave **now**.
- I saw that movie **last year**.

Putting an adverb that tells us when at the end of a sentence is a neutral position, but these adverbs can be put in other positions to give a different emphasis. All adverbs that tell us when can be placed at the beginning of the sentence to emphasize the time element. Some can also be put before the main verb in formal writing, while others cannot occupy that position.

Examples

- **Later** Goldilocks ate some porridge. (the time is important)
- Goldilocks **later** ate some porridge. (this is more formal, like a policeman's report)
- Goldilocks ate some porridge **later**. (this is neutral, no particular emphasis)

Adverbs that tell us for how long

Adverbs that tell us for how long are also usually placed at the end of the sentence.

Examples

- She stayed in the Bears' house **all day**.
- My mother lived in France **for a year**.
- I have been going to this school **since 1996**.

In these adverbial phrases that tell us for how long, *for* is always followed by an expression of duration, while *since* is always followed by an expression of a point in time.

Examples

- I stayed in Switzerland **for three days**.
- I am going on vacation **for a week**.
- I have been riding horses **for several years**.
- The French monarchy lasted **for several centuries**.
- I have not seen you **since Monday**.
- Jim has been working here **since 1997**.
- There has not been a more exciting discovery **since last century**.

Adverbs that tell us how often

Adverbs that tell us how often express the frequency of an action. They are usually placed before the main verb but after auxiliary verbs (such as *be, have, may, & must*). The only exception is when the main verb is "to be", in which case the adverb goes after the main verb.

Examples

- I **often** eat vegetarian food.
- He **never** drinks milk.
- You must **always** fasten your seat belt.
- I am **seldom** late.
- He **rarely** lies.

Many adverbs that express frequency can also be placed at either the beginning or the end of the sentence, although some cannot be. When they are placed in these alternate positions, the meaning of the adverb is much stronger.

Adverb that can be used in two positions	Stronger position	Weaker position
frequently	I visit France **frequently**.	I **frequently** visit France.
generally	**Generally**, I don't like spicy foods.	I **generally** don't like spicy foods.

Adverb that can be used in two positions	Stronger position	Weaker position
normally	I listen to classical music **normally**.	I **normally** listen to classical music.
occasionally	I go to the opera **occasionally**.	I **occasionally** go to the opera.
often	**Often**, I jog in the morning.	I **often** jog in the morning.
regularly	I come to this museum **regularly**.	I **regularly** come to this museum.
sometimes	I get up very early **sometimes**.	I **sometimes** get up very early.
usually	I enjoy being with children **usually**.	I **usually** enjoy being with children.

Some other adverbs that tell us how often express the exact number of times an action happens or happened. These adverbs are usually placed at the end of the sentence.

Examples

- This magazine is published **monthly**.
- He visits his mother **once a week**.
- I work **five days a week**.
- I saw the movie **seven times**.

Using Yet

Yet is used in questions and in negative sentences to indicate that something that has not happened or may not have happened but is expected to happen. It is placed at the end of the sentence or after *not*.

Examples

- Have you finished your work **yet**? (= simple request for information)
- No, not **yet**. (= simple negative answer)
- They haven't met him **yet**. (= simple negative statement)
- Haven't you finished **yet**? (= expressing surprise)

Using Still

Still expresses continuity. In positive sentences it is placed before the main verb and after auxiliary verbs such as *be, have, might, will*. If the main verb is *to be*, then place *still* after it rather than before. In questions, *still* goes before the main verb.

Examples

- She is **still** waiting for you.
- Jim might **still** want some.
- Do you **still** work for the BBC?
- Are you **still** here?
- I am **still** hungry.

Order of adverbs of time

If you need to use more than one adverb of time in a sentence, use them in this order:

1: how long 2: how often 3: when

Examples

- 1 + 2 : I work (1) **for five hours** (2) **every day**
- 2 + 3 : The magazine was published (2) **weekly** (3) **last year**.
- 1 + 3 : I was abroad (1) **for two months** (3) **last year**.
- 1 + 2 + 3 : She worked in a hospital (1) **for two days** (2) **every week** (3) **last year**.

Adverbs of place

Adverbs of place tell us where something happens. They are usually placed after the main verb or after the clause that they modify. Adverbs of place do not modify adjectives or other adverbs.

Examples

- John looked **around** but he couldn't see the monkey.
- I searched **everywhere** I could think of.
- I'm going **back** to school.
- Come **in**!
- They built a house **nearby**.
- She took the child **outside**.

Here and There

Here and *there* are common adverbs of place. They give a location relative to the speaker. With verbs of movement, *here* means "towards or with the speaker" and *there* means "away from, or not with the speaker".

Sentence	Meaning
Come here!	Come towards me.
The table is in here.	Come with me; we will go see it together.
Put it there.	Put it in a place away from me.
The table is in there.	Go in; you can see it by yourself.

Here and *there* are combined with prepositions to make many common adverbial phrases.

Examples

- What are you doing **up there**?
- Come **over here** and look at what I found!
- The baby is hiding **down there** under the table.
- I wonder how my driver's license got stuck **under here**.

Here and *there* are placed at the beginning of the sentence in exclamations or when emphasis is needed. They are followed by the verb if the subject is a noun or by a pronoun if the subject is a pronoun.

Examples

- **Here** comes the bus!
- **There** goes the bell!

- **There** it is!
- **Here** they are!

Adverbs of place that are also prepositions

Many adverbs of place can also be used as prepositions. When used as prepositions, they must be followed by a noun.

Word	Used as an adverb of place, modifying a verb	Used as a preposition
around	The marble **rolled around** in my hand.	I am wearing a necklace **around my neck**.
behind	Hurry! You are **getting behind**.	Let's hide **behind the shed**.
down	Mary **fell down**.	John made his way carefully **down the cliff**.
in	We decided to **drop in** on Jake.	I dropped the letter **in the mailbox**.
off	Let's **get off** at the next stop.	The wind blew the flowers **off the tree**.
on	We **rode on** for several more hours.	Please put the books **on the table**.

Word	Used as an adverb of place, modifying a verb	Used as a preposition
over	He **turned over** and went back to sleep.	I think I will hang the picture **over my bed**.

Adverbs of place ending in -where

Adverbs of place that end in -where express the idea of location without specifying a specific location or direction.

Examples

- I would like to go **somewhere** warm for my vacation.
- Is there **anywhere** I can find a perfect plate of spaghetti around here?
- I have **nowhere** to go.
- I keep running in to Sally **everywhere**!

Adverbs of place ending in -wards

Adverbs of place that end in -wards express movement in a particular direction.

Examples

- Cats don't usually walk **backwards**.
- The ship sailed **westwards**.
- The balloon drifted **upwards**.
- We will keep walking **homewards** until we arrive.

Be careful: *Towards* is a preposition, not an adverb, so it is always followed by a noun or a pronoun.

Examples

- He walked **towards the car**.
- She ran **towards me**.

Adverbs of place expressing both movement & location

Some adverbs of place express both movement & location at the same time.

Examples

- The child went **indoors**.
- He lived and worked **abroad**.
- Water always flows **downhill**.
- The wind pushed us **sideways**.

How to Pronounce Dates and Numbers[1]

Dates
In English, we can say dates either with the day before the month, or the month before the day:
"The first of January" / **"January the first"**.

Remember to use ordinal numbers for dates in English.
(The first, the second, the third, the fourth, the fifth, the twenty-second, the thirty-first etc.)

Years
For years up until 2000, separate the four numbers into two pairs of two:
1965 = **"nineteen sixty-five"**
1871 = **"eighteen seventy-one"**
1999 = **"nineteen ninety-nine"**

For the decade 2001 – 2010, you say "two thousand and —-" when speaking British English:
2001 = **"two thousand and one"**
2009 = **"two thousand and nine"**

However, from 2010 onwards you have a choice.
For example, 2012 can be either **"two thousand and twelve"** or **"twenty twelve"**.

---

[1] Excerpted from http://www.english-at-home.com/pronunciation/saying-dates-and-numbers-in-english/

Large numbers

Divide the number into units of hundreds and thousands:

400,000 = "**four hundred thousand**" (no **s** plural)

If the number includes a smaller number, use "and" in British English:

450,000 = "**four hundred and fifty thousand**"

400,360 = "**four hundred thousand and three hundred and sixty**"

Fractions, ratios and percentages

½ = "**one half**"

1/3 = "**one third**"

¼ = "**one quarter**"

1/5 = "**one fifth**"

1/ 6 = "**one sixth**"

3/5 = "**three fifths**"

1.5% = "**one point five percent**"

0.3% = "**nought / zero point three percent**"

2:1 = "**two to one**"

Saying 0

Depending on the context, we can pronounce zero in different ways:

2-0 (football) = "**Two nil**"

30 – 0 (tennis) = "**Thirty love**"

604 7721 (phone number) = "**six oh four…**"

0.4 (a number) = "**nought point four**" or "**zero point four**"

0C (temperature) = "**zero degrees**"

Talking about calculations in English

+ (**plus**)

= (equals / makes)
2 + 1 = 3 ("two plus one equals / makes three")
– (minus / take away)
5 – 3 = 2 ("five minus three equals two" / "five take away three equals two")
x (multiplied by / times)
2 x 3 = 6 ("two multiplied by three equals six" / "two times three equals six")
/ (divided by)
6 / 3 = 2 ("six divided by three equals two")

Linking Between Words [2]

When you listen to spoken English, it very often sounds smooth, rather than staccato. One of the ways we achieve this is to link sounds between words.

Using a /r/ sound

For example, we use a /r/ sound between two vowel sounds (when one word ends with a vowel sound of 'uh' (as in the final sound of banana); 'er' (as in the final sound of murder); and 'or' (as in the final sound of or). The /r/ sound happens when the next word starts with a vowel.

A matter of opinion = "A matte – rof opinion"

Murder is a crime = "Murde – ris a crime"

For example = "Fo – rexample".

Using a /w/ sound

We use a /w/ sound when the first word ends in a 'oo' sound (as in you); or an 'oh' sound (as in no) or an 'ow' sound (as in now)

Who are your best friends? = "Who – ware – your ….."

---

[2] Excerpted from http://www.english-at-home.com/pronunciation/linking-between-words/

No you don't = "No – wyou don't"

Now I know = "No – wI – know"

Using a /j/ sound

If you say the words "I" and "am" quickly, the sound between is a /ya/ sound. You can probably feel the sound at the back of your mouth, as the bottom of your mouth comes up to meet the top. The /j/ sound can link words which end with an /ai/ sound (I) or an /ey/ sound (may).

I am English = I – yam English

May I go? = May – jI go?

Consonant and vowel

When one word ends with a consonant (and the next begins with a vowel sound) use the final consonant to link.

An + apple sounds like a – napple.

Don't add an extra vowel after that consonant. So it's a – napple, rather than a – n – a apple.

Here are some more examples of consonants linking to vowels:

At all = "A – tall"

Speak up = "Spea – kup"

Right away = "Righ – taway"

Leave it = "Lea – vit"

School again = "Schoo – lagain"

Introduction to the Arabic Language

Arabic (Arabic: الْعَرَبِية, al-'arabiyyah [alˤaraˈbijja] or Arabic: عربى, عـــربي 'arabī [ˈˤarabiː] belongs to the Semitic branch of the Afroasiatic family. Arabic is a Central Semitic language, closely related to Aramaic, Hebrew, Ugaritic and Phoenician. Arabic is the only surviving member of the Ancient North Arabian dialect group attested in pre-Islamic Arabic inscriptions dating back to the 4th century.[3]

Standard Arabic is distinct from and more conservative than all of the spoken varieties, and the two exist in a state known as diglossia, used side-by-side for different societal functions. It is the Classical Arabic language of the 6th century and its modern descendants excluding Maltese. Arabic is spoken in a wide arc stretching across Western Asia, North Africa, and the Horn of Africa.

The literary language, called Modern Standard Arabic or Literary Arabic, is the only official form of Arabic. It is used in most written documents as well as in formal spoken occasions, such as lectures and news broadcasts.

Some of the spoken varieties are mutually unintelligible,[4] both written and orally, and the varieties as a whole constitute a sociolinguistic language. This means that on purely linguistic

---

[3] *Versteegh, Kees (1997), The Arabic Language, Edinburgh University Press, ISBN 90-04-17702-7 (1997:33)*

[4] "Arabic language." *Encyclopædia Britannica.* 2009. Encyclopædia Britannica Online. Retrieved on 29 July 2009.

grounds they would likely be considered to constitute more than one language, but are commonly grouped together as a single language for political or religious reasons. If considered multiple languages, it is unclear how many languages there would be, as the spoken varieties form a dialect chain with no clear boundaries. If Arabic is considered a single language, it is perhaps spoken by as many as 422 million speakers (native and non-native) in the Arab world,[5] making it one of the six most-spoken languages in the world. If considered separate languages, the most-spoken variety would most likely be Egyptian Arabic[6] with 89 million native speakers[7] — still greater than any other Afroasiatic language. Arabic also is a liturgical language of 1.6 billion Muslims.[8] It is one of six official languages of the United Nations.

The modern written language (Modern Standard Arabic) is derived from the language of the Quran (known as Classical Arabic or Quranic Arabic). It is widely taught in schools and

---

[5] *"World Arabic Language Day"*. *UNESCO. 18 December 2014. Retrieved 12 February 2014. http://www.unesco.org/new/en/unesco/events/prizes-and-celebrations/celebrations/international-days/world-arabic-language-day/*

[6] Egyptian Arabic at *Ethnologue* (18th ed., 2015)

[7] *The World Factbook"*. *www.cia.gov. Retrieved 2015-09-14.*

[8] *Executive Summary"*. *Future of the Global Muslim Population. Pew Research Center. Retrieved 22 December 2011.*

"Table: Muslim Population by Country | Pew Research Center's Religion & Public Life Project". *Features.pewforum.org. 2011-01-27. Retrieved 2014-05-18.*

universities, and is used to varying degrees in workplaces, government, and the media. The two formal varieties are grouped together as Literary Arabic, which is the official language of 26 states and the liturgical language of Islam. Modern Standard Arabic largely follows the grammatical standards of Quranic Arabic and uses much of the same vocabulary. However, it has discarded some grammatical constructions and vocabulary that no longer have any counterpart in the spoken varieties, and has adopted certain new constructions and vocabulary from the spoken varieties. Much of the new vocabulary is used to denote concepts that have arisen in the post-Quranic era, especially in modern times.

Arabic has influenced many languages around the globe throughout its history. Some of the most influenced languages are Persian, Turkish, Urdu, Kurdish, Somali, Swahili, Bosnian, Kazakh, Bengali, Hindi, Malay, Indonesian, Tigrinya, Pashto, Punjabi, Tagalog, Sindhi and Hausa. During the Middle Ages, Literary Arabic was a major vehicle of culture in Europe, especially in science, mathematics and philosophy. As a result, many European languages have also borrowed many words from it. Many words of Arabic origin are also found in ancient languages like Latin and Greek. Arabic influence, mainly in vocabulary, is seen in Romance languages, particularly Spanish, Catalan, Galician, Portuguese, and Sicilian, owing to both the proximity of Christian European and Muslim Arab civilizations and 800 years of Arabic culture and language in the Iberian Peninsula, referred to in Arabic as al-Andalus.

Arabic has also borrowed words from many languages, including Hebrew, Aramaic, Greek, Persian and Syriac in early centuries, Kurdish in medieval times and contemporary European languages in modern times, mostly English and French.

Arabic is written with the Arabic alphabet, which is an abjad script and is written from right-to-left although the spoken varieties are sometimes written in ASCII Latin from left-to-right with no standardized forms.

Classical, Modern Standard and Spoken Arabic

Arabic usually designates one of three main variants: Classical Arabic, Modern Standard Arabic and colloquial or dialectal Arabic. Classical Arabic is the language found in the Quran, used from the period of Pre-Islamic Arabia to that of the Abbasid Caliphate. Theoretically, Classical Arabic is considered normative, according to the syntactic and grammatical norms laid down by classical grammarians (such as Sibawayh) and the vocabulary defined in classical dictionaries (such as the Lisān al-'Arab). In practice, however, modern authors almost never write in pure Classical Arabic, instead using a literary language with its own grammatical norms and vocabulary, commonly known as Modern Standard Arabic (MSA).

MSA is the variety used in most current, printed Arabic publications, spoken by some of the Arabic media across North Africa, the Horn of Africa and the Middle East, and understood by most educated Arabic speakers. "Literary Arabic" and "Standard Arabic" (فُصْحَى fuṣḥá) are less strictly defined terms that may refer to Modern Standard Arabic or Classical Arabic.

Some of the differences between Classical Arabic (CA) and Modern Standard Arabic (MSA) are as follows:

Certain grammatical constructions of CA that have no counterpart in any modern dialect (e.g., the energetic mood) are almost never used in Modern Standard Arabic.

No modern spoken variety of Arabic has case distinctions. As a result, MSA is generally composed without case distinctions in mind, and the proper cases are added after the fact, when necessary. Because most case endings are noted using final short vowels, which are normally left unwritten in the Arabic script, it is unnecessary to determine the proper case of most words. The practical result of this is that MSA, like English and Standard Chinese, is written in a strongly determined word order and alternative orders that were used in CA for emphasis are rare. In addition, because of the lack of case marking in the spoken varieties, most speakers cannot consistently use the correct endings in extemporaneous speech. As a result, spoken MSA tends to drop or regularize the endings except when reading from a prepared text.

The numeral system in CA is complex and heavily tied in with the case system. This system is never used in MSA, even in the most formal of circumstances; instead, a significantly simplified system is used, approximating the system of the conservative spoken varieties.

MSA uses much Classical vocabulary (e.g., dhahaba 'to go') that is not present in the spoken varieties. In addition, MSA has borrowed or coined a large number of terms for concepts that did not exist in Quranic times, and MSA continues to evolve.[27] Some words have been borrowed from other languages — notice that transliteration mainly indicates spelling and not real pronunciation (e.g., فيلــــم fīlm 'film' or ديموقراطيــــة dīmūqrāṭiyyah 'democracy').

However, the current preference is to avoid direct borrowings, preferring to either use loan translations (e.g., فــرع far‘ 'branch', also used for the branch of a company or organization; جنـاح jināḥ 'wing', is also used for the wing of an airplane, building, air force, etc.), or to coin new words using forms within existing roots (اســـتماتة istimātah 'apoptosis', using the root موت m/w/t 'death' put into the Xth form, or جامعة jāmi‘ah 'university', based on جمع jama‘a 'to gather, unite'; جمهورية jumhūriyyah 'republic', based on جمهور jumhūr 'multitude'). An earlier tendency was to repurpose older words; that has fallen into disuse (e.g., هاتف hātif 'telephone' < 'invisible caller (in Sufism)'; جريـدة jarīdah 'newspaper' < 'palm-leaf stalk').

Colloquial or dialectal Arabic refers to the many national or regional varieties which constitute the everyday spoken language. Colloquial Arabic has many regional variants; geographically distant varieties usually differ enough to be mutually unintelligible, and some linguists consider them distinct languages.[28] The varieties are typically unwritten. They are often used in informal spoken media, such as soap operas and talk shows,[29] as well as occasionally in certain forms of written media such as poetry and printed advertising.

The only variety of modern Arabic to have acquired official language status is Maltese, which is spoken in (predominately Roman Catholic) Malta and written with the Latin script. It is descended from Classical Arabic through Siculo-Arabic, but is not mutually intelligible with any other variety of Arabic. Most linguists list it as a separate language rather than as a dialect of Arabic. Historically, Algerian Arabic was taught in French Algeria under the name darija.

Even during Muhammad's lifetime, there were dialects of spoken Arabic. Muhammad spoke in the dialect of Mecca, in the western Arabian peninsula, and it was in this dialect that the Quran was written down. However, the dialects of the eastern Arabian peninsula were considered the most prestigious at the time, so the language of the Quran was ultimately converted to follow the eastern phonology. It is this phonology that underlies the modern pronunciation of Classical Arabic. The phonological differences between these two dialects account for some of the complexities of Arabic writing, most notably the writing of the glottal stop or hamzah (which was preserved in the eastern dialects but lost in western speech) and the use of alif maqṣūrah (representing a sound preserved in the western dialects but merged with ā in eastern speech).

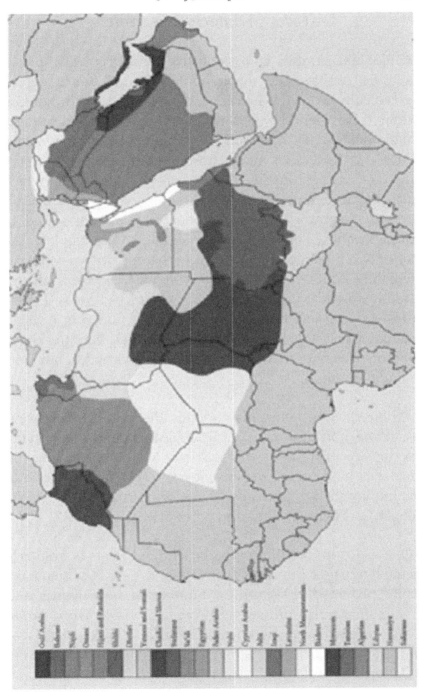

Different Dialects of Arabic

Colloquial Arabic is a collective term for the spoken varieties of Arabic used throughout the Arab world, which differ radically from the literary language. The main dialectal division is between the varieties within and outside of the Arabian peninsula, followed by that between sedentary varieties and the much more conservative Bedouin varieties. All of the varieties outside of the Arabian peninsula (which include the large majority of speakers) have a large number of features in common with each other that are not found in Classical Arabic. This has led researchers to postulate the existence of a prestige koine dialect in the one or two centuries immediately following the Arab conquest, whose features eventually spread to all of the newly conquered areas. (These features are present to varying degrees inside the Arabian peninsula. Generally, the Arabian peninsula varieties have much more diversity than the non-peninsula varieties, but have been understudied.)

Within the non-peninsula varieties, the largest difference is between the non-Egyptian North African dialects (especially Moroccan Arabic) and the others. Moroccan Arabic in particular is hardly comprehensible to Arabic speakers east of Libya (although the converse is not true, in part due to the popularity of Egyptian films and other media).

One factor in the differentiation of the dialects is influence from the languages previously spoken in the areas, which have typically provided a significant number of new words and have sometimes also influenced pronunciation or word order; however, a much more significant factor for most dialects is, as among Romance languages, retention (or change of meaning) of different classical forms. Thus Iraqi aku, Levantine fīh and

North African kayən all mean 'there is', and all come from Classical Arabic forms (yakūn, fīhi, kā'in respectively), but now sound very different.

Examples of Dialectical Differences

Variety	I love reading a lot	When I went to the library	I didn't find this old book	I wanted to read a book about the history of women in France
Literary Arabic in Arabic script (dialects are written in other non-standardized spellings)	أنا أحبّ القراءة كثيراً	عندما ذهبت إلى المكتبة	لم أجد هٰذا الكتاب القديم	كنت أردت أن أقرأ كتاباً عن تاريخ المرأة في فرنسا
Classical Arabic (liturgical or poetic only)	ʔana: ʔuħib:u l-qira:ʔata kaθi:ra:	ʕindama: ðahabtu ʔila: l-maktabah	lam ʔaʝidu ha:ða: l-kita:ba l-qadi:m	kuntu ʔaradtu ʔan ʔaqraʔa kita:ban ʕan ta:ri:xi l-marʔati fi: faransa:
Modern Standard Arabic	ʔana(:) ʔuħibb al-qira:ʔa kaθi:ran	ʕindama(:) ðahabtu ʔila: l-maktaba	lam ʔaʝid ha:ða(:) l-kita:b al-qadi:m	kuntu ʔaradtu ʔan ʔaqraʔ kita:b ʕan

				ta:ri:x al-mar?a fi: faransa(:)
Yemeni Arabic (Sanaa)	'ʔana bajn a'ħibb el-ge'ra:je 'gawi	'law ma 'sert sa'la: el-'maktabe	ma le'ge:t-ʃ 'ðajje al-ke'ta:b el-ga'di:m	kont 'aʃti 'ʔagra ke'ta:b ʕan ta'ri:x al-'mare wastˤ fa'ra:nsa
Gulf Arabic (Kuwait)	ʔa:na wa:yed aħibb agra:	lamman reħt al-maktaba	ma lige:t hal keta:b al-gadi:m	kent abi: agra keta:b an tari:x el-ħari:m eb fransa
Gilit Mesopotamian (Baghdad?)	'a:ni a'ħibb el-q'ra:ja 'kulliʃ	'lamman 'reħit lel-maktaba	ma li'ge:t ha:ða l-keta:b al-qadi:m	redet aqra keta:b ʕan tari:x al-niswan eb-fransa
Hijazi Arabic (Medina)	'ana marra a'ħubb al-gira:ja	'lamma ruħt al-'maktaba	ma ligi:t ha:da l-kita:b al-gadi:m	kunt abɣa agra kita:b ʕan tari:x al-ħari:m fi faransa
Western Syrian Arabic (Damascus)	ʔana kti:r b'ħəbb lˤ-ʔra:je	'lamma 'rəħt ʕal-'maktabe	ma laʔe:t ha-l-ᵊk'ta:b lˤ-ʔ'di:m	ka:n 'baddi ʔra kta:b ʕan ta'ri:x ᵊl-'mara bˤ-'fra:nsa
Lebanese Arabic (Beyrut?)	kti:r bħibb il-ʔi're:je	'lamma 'reħit ʕal-'maktabe	ma lʔe:t ha-l-ik'te:b le-	ke:n 'baddi ʔra kte:b ʕan te'ri:x

			ʔ'di:m	il-'mara bi-'fra:nsa
Urban Palestinian (Jerusalem)	'ʔana ba'ħebb l-ᵊʔ'ra:je kti:r	'lamma 'ruħᵊt ʕal-'maktabe	ma la'ʔe:tᵊʃ ha-l-ᵊk'ta:b ᵊl-ʔa'di:m	ka:n 'beddi 'ʔaʔra kta:b ʕan ta'ri:x ᵊl-'mara fi f'ransa
Rural Palestinian (West Bank)	'ʔana ba'ħebb l-ᵊk'ra:je kθi:r	'lamma 'ruħᵊt ʕal-'matʃtabe	ma la'ke:tᵊʃ ha-l-ᵊtʃ'ta:b ᵊl-ka'di:m	ka:n 'beddi 'ʔakra tʃta:b ʕan ta'ri:x ᵊl-'mara fi f'ransa
Egyptian (metropolitan)	ana baħebb el-ʔera:ja ʔawi	'lamma 'roht el-mak'taba	ma-l'ʔet-ʃ l-ke'ta:b el-ʔa'di:m da	'ana 'kont-e 'ʕawz-'aʔra k'ta:b ʕan ta'ri:x el-set'ta:t fe fa'ransa
Libyan Arabic (Tripoli?)	ana nħəb il-gra:ja halba	lamma mʃe:t lil-maktba	malge:tiʃ ha-li-kta:b lə-gdi:m	kunt nibi nagra kta:b ʔle: tari:x ə-nsawi:n fi fra:nsa
Tunisian (Tunis)	nħɪb lɪqra:jæ barʃæ	wæqtɪlli mʃi:t lilmæktbæ	mæl-qi:tʃ hæ-lɪktɛ:b lɪqdi:m	kʊnt nħɪb næqræ kte:b ʕlæ tɛrix lɪmræ fi fra:nsæ
Algerian (Algiers?)	e:na nħebb l-qra:ja	ki ruħt l il-maktaba	ma-lqi:t-ʃ ha l-kte:b l-qdi:m	kunt ħa:b naqra kte:b ʕala tari:x l-

	bezzef			mra fi fra:nsa
Moroccan (Rabat?)	ana ʕziz ʕlija bzzaf nqra	melli mʃit l-lmaktaba	ma-lqi:t-ʃ had l-ktab l-qdim	kent baɣi nqra ktab ʕla tarix l-mra f-fransa
Maltese (Valetta)	ɪnħɔpː neʔre ħefne	mɐte mɔrt ɪl-lɪbrɛrɪje	mɐ sɪbtʃ dɐn ɪl-ktiɛp ʔedɪm	rɪdt neʔre ktiep dwer l-ɪstɔrje tel-mɐre fɪ frɐntse

Koine

The following are some of the characteristic features of the koine that underlies all of the modern dialects outside the Arabian peninsula. [9]Although many other features are common to most or all of these varieties, Ferguson believes that these features in particular are unlikely to have evolved independently more than once or twice and together suggest the existence of the koine:

Loss of the dual (grammatical number) except on nouns, with consistent plural agreement (cf. feminine singular agreement in plural inanimates).

Change of a to i in many affixes (e.g., non-past-tense prefixes ti- yi- ni-; wi- 'and'; il- 'the'; feminine -it in the construct state).

Loss of third-weak verbs ending in w (which merge with verbs ending in y).

Reformation of geminate verbs, e.g., ḥalaltu 'I untied' → ḥalēt(u).

Conversion of separate words lī 'to me', laka 'to you', etc. into indirect-object clitic suffixes.

Certain changes in the cardinal number system, e.g., khamsat ayyām 'five days' → kham(a)s tiyyām, where certain words have a special plural with prefixed t.

---

[9] *Ferguson, Charles (1959), "The Arabic Koine", Language* **35** *(4): 616–630,* <u>*doi*</u>*:10.2307/410601*

Loss of the feminine elative (comparative).

Adjective plurals of the form kibār 'big' → kubār.

Change of nisba suffix -iyy > i.

Certain lexical items, e.g., jāb 'bring' < jāʾa bi- 'come with'; shāf 'see'; ēsh 'what' (or similar) < ayyu shayʾ 'which thing'; illi (relative pronoun).

Merger of /ẓ/ and /ð̣/.

Dialect groups

Egyptian Arabic is spoken by around 53 million in Egypt (55 million worldwide).[10] It is one of the most understood varieties of Arabic, due in large part to the widespread distribution of Egyptian films and television shows throughout the Arabic-speaking world

Levantine Arabic includes North Levantine Arabic, South Levantine Arabic and Cypriot Arabic. It is spoken by about 21 million people in Lebanon, Syria, Jordan, Palestinian Territories, Israel, Cyprus and Turkey.

Maghrebi Arabic, also called "Darija" spoken by about 70 million people in Morocco, Algeria, Tunisia, Libya and Malta. It is very hard to understand for Arabic speakers from the Mashriq or Mesopotamia, the easiest being Libyan Arabic and the hardest Moroccan Arabic and Maltese language (which is close to Tunisian Arabic) . The others such as Algerian Arabic can be considered "in between".

Maltese, spoken on the island of Malta, is the only dialect to have established itself as a fully separate language, with independent literary norms. Sicilian Arabic, spoken on the island of Sicily until the 14th century, developed into Maltese in Malta. In the course of its history the language has adopted numerous loanwords, phonetic and phonological features, and even some grammatical patterns, from Italian, Sicilian and English. It is also the only Semitic language written in the Latin script. Furthermore, Maltese or Sicilian Arabic are closely

---

[10] *Arabic, Egyptian Spoken (18th ed.). Ethnologue. 2006.*

related to Tunisian Arabic due to the cultural and historical ties between Tunisia and Malta,[11] and the languages are partially mutually intelligible.[12]

Mesopotamian Arabic, spoken by about 7 million people in Iraq (where it is called "Aamiyah"), eastern Syria and southwestern Iran (Khuzestan).

Sudanese Arabic is spoken by 17 million people in Sudan and some parts of southern Egypt. Sudanese Arabic is quite distinct from the dialect of its neighbor to the north; rather, the Sudanese have a dialect similar to the Hijazi dialect.

Gulf Arabic, spoken by around four million people, predominantly in Kuwait, Bahrain, some parts of Oman, eastern Saudi Arabia coastal areas and some parts of UAE and Qatar. Also spoken in Iran's Bushehr and Hormozgan provinces. Although Gulf Arabic is spoken in Qatar, most Qatari citizens speak Najdi Arabic (Bedawi).

Yemeni Arabic spoken in Yemen, Somalia, Djibouti and southern Saudi Arabia by 15 million people. Similar to Gulf Arabic.

---

[11] Borg and Azzopardi-Alexander *Maltese* (1997:xiii) "The immediate source for the Arabic vernacular spoken in Malta was Muslim Sicily, but its ultimate origin appears to have been Tunisia. In fact Maltese displays some areal traits typical of Maghrebine Arabic, although during the past eight hundred years of independent evolution it has drifted apart from Tunisian Arabic".

[12] Borg and Azzopardi-Alexander *Maltese* (1997:xiii).

Najdi Arabic, spoken by around 10 million people, mainly spoken in Najd, central and northern Saudi Arabia. Most Qatari citizens speak Najdi Arabic (Bedawi).

Hejazi Arabic (6 million speakers), spoken in Hijaz, western Saudi Arabia

Hassaniya Arabic (3 million speakers), spoken in Mauritania, Western Sahara, some parts of northern Mali, southern Morocco and south-western Algeria.

Bahrani Arabic (600,000 speakers), spoken by Bahrani Shi'ah in Bahrain and Qatif, the dialect exhibits many big differences from Gulf Arabic. It is also spoken to a lesser extent in Oman.

Judeo-Arabic dialects - these are the dialects spoken by the Jews that had lived or continue to live in the Arab World. As Jewish migration to Israel took hold, the language did not thrive and is now considered endangered.

Central Asian Arabic, spoken in Uzbekistan, Tajikistan and Afghanistan, is highly endangered.

Samaritan Arabic, spoken by only several hundred in the Nablus region.

Shirvani Arabic, spoken in Azerbaijan and Dagestan until the 1930s, now extinct.

Andalusian Arabic, spoken in Spain and Portugal until the 16th century.

Phonology

The "colloquial" spoken varieties of Arabic are learned at home and constitute the native languages of Arabic speakers. "Formal" Literary Arabic (usually specifically Modern Standard Arabic) is learned at school; although many speakers have a native-like command of the language, it is technically not the native language of any speakers. Both varieties can be both written and spoken, although the colloquial varieties are rarely written down and the formal variety is spoken mostly in formal circumstances, e.g., in radio broadcasts, formal lectures, parliamentary discussions and to some extent between speakers of different colloquial varieties. Even when the literary language is spoken, however, it is normally only spoken in its pure form when reading a prepared text out loud. When speaking extemporaneously (i.e. making up the language on the spot, as in a normal discussion among people), speakers tend to deviate somewhat from the strict literary language in the direction of the colloquial varieties. In fact, there is a continuous range of "in-between" spoken varieties: from nearly pure Modern Standard Arabic (MSA), to a form that still uses MSA grammar and vocabulary but with significant colloquial influence, to a form of the colloquial language that imports a number of words and grammatical constructions in MSA, to a form that is close to pure colloquial but with the "rough edges" (the most noticeably "vulgar" or non-Classical aspects) smoothed out, to pure colloquial. The particular variant (or register) used depends on the social class and education level of the speakers involved and the level of formality of the speech situation. Often it will vary within a single encounter, e.g., moving from nearly pure MSA to a more mixed language in the process of a radio interview, as the interviewee becomes more comfortable with the interviewer.

This type of variation is characteristic of the diglossia that exists throughout the Arabic-speaking world.

Literary Arabic

Although Modern Standard Arabic (MSA) is a unitary language, its pronunciation varies somewhat from country to country and from region to region within a country. The variation in individual "accents" of MSA speakers tends to mirror corresponding variations in the colloquial speech of the speakers in question, but with the distinguishing characteristics moderated somewhat. Note that it is important in descriptions of "Arabic" phonology to distinguish between pronunciation of a given colloquial (spoken) dialect and the pronunciation of MSA by these same speakers. Although they are related, they are not the same. For example, the phoneme that derives from Proto-Semitic /g/ has many different pronunciations in the modern spoken varieties, e.g., [dʒ ~ ʒ ~ j ~ gʲ ~ g]. Speakers whose native variety has either [dʒ] or [ʒ] will use the same pronunciation when speaking MSA. Even speakers from Cairo, whose native Egyptian Arabic has [g], normally use [g] when speaking MSA. The [j] of Persian Gulf speakers is the only variant pronunciation which isn't found in MSA; [dʒ~ʒ] is used instead.

Another example:

Many colloquial varieties are known for a type of vowel harmony in which the presence of an "emphatic consonant" triggers backed allophones of nearby vowels (especially of the low vowels /aː/, which are backed to [ɑ(ː)] in these circumstances and very often fronted to [æ(ː)] in all other circumstances). In many spoken varieties, the backed or "emphatic" vowel allophones spread a fair distance in both directions from the triggering consonant; in some varieties (most notably Egyptian Arabic), the "emphatic" allophones spread throughout the entire word, usually including prefixes and suffixes, even at a distance of several syllables from the triggering consonant. Speakers of colloquial varieties with this vowel harmony tend to introduce it into their MSA pronunciation as well, but usually with a lesser degree of spreading than in the colloquial varieties. (For example, speakers of colloquial varieties with extremely long-distance harmony may allow a moderate, but not extreme, amount of spreading of the harmonic allophones in their MSA speech, while speakers of colloquial varieties with moderate-distance harmony may only harmonize immediately adjacent vowels in MSA.)

Vowels

Modern Standard Arabic has six pure vowels, with short /a i u/ and corresponding long vowels /aː iː uː/. There are also two diphthongs: /aj/ and /aw/.

The pronunciation of the vowels differs from speaker to speaker, in a way that tends to reflect the pronunciation of the corresponding colloquial variety. Nonetheless, there are some common trends. Most noticeable is the differing pronunciation of /a/ and /aː/, which tend towards fronted [æ(ː)], [a(ː)] or [ɛ(ː)] in most situations, but a back [ɑ(ː)] in the neighborhood of emphatic consonants. Some accents and dialects, such as those of the Hijaz, have central [ä(ː)] in all situations. The vowels /u/ and /i/ are often affected somewhat in emphatic neighborhoods as well, with generally more back or centralized allophones, but the differences are less great than for the low vowels. The pronunciation of short /u/ and /i/ tends towards [ʊ~o] and [ɪ~e] in many dialects.

The definition of both "emphatic" and "neighborhood" vary in ways that reflect (to some extent) corresponding variations in the spoken dialects. Generally, the consonants triggering "emphatic" allophones are the pharyngealized consonants /tˤ dˤ sˤ ðˤ/; /q/; and /r/, if not followed immediately by /i(ː)/. Frequently, the uvular fricatives /x ɣ/ also trigger emphatic allophones; occasionally also the pharyngeal consonants /ʕ ħ/ (the former more than the latter). Many dialects have multiple emphatic allophones of each vowel, depending on the particular nearby consonants. In most MSA accents, emphatic coloring of vowels is limited to vowels immediately adjacent to a triggering consonant, although in some it spreads a bit farther: e.g., وقت waqt [wɑqt] 'time'; وطن waṭan [watˤɑn] 'homeland'; وسط المدينـــة waṣṭ al-madīnah [wæstˤal-mædiːnɐ] 'downtown' (sometimes [wɑstˤal-mædiːnæ] or similar).

In a non-emphatic environment, the vowel /a/ in the diphthong /aj/ tends to be fronted even more than elsewhere, often pronounced [æj] or [ɛj]: hence ســيف sayf [sajf ~ sæjf ~ sɛjf] 'sword' but صــيف ṣayf [sˤɑjf] 'summer'. However, in accents with no emphatic allophones of /a/ (e.g., in the Hijaz), the pronunciation [äj] occurs in all situations

Consonants

		Labial	Interdental		Alveolar, Dental		Palatal	Velar	Uvular	Pharyngeal	Glottal
Consonant phonemes of Standard Arabic											
			plain	emp.	emp.	plain					
Nasal		m				n					
Stop	voiceless	b			tˤ	t		k	q		ʔ
	voiced				dˤ3	d	ʒ~dʒ~ʝ~gʲ~g				
Fricative	voiceless	f	θ		sˤ	s	ʃ	x~χ[61]		ħ	h
	voiced		ð	ðˤ~zˤ		z		ɣ~ʁ		ʕ	
Approximant						l	j	w			
Trill						r					

The phoneme /ʒ~dʒ~ʝ~gʲ~g/ is represented by the Arabic letter *jīm* (ج) and has many standard pronunciations. [dʒ] is characteristic of north Algeria, Iraq, also in most of the Arabian peninsula but with an allophonic [ʒ] in some positions; [ʒ] occurs in most of the Levant and most North Africa; and [g] is used in most of Egypt and some regions in Yemen and Oman. Generally this corresponds with the pronunciation in the colloquial dialects.[62] In some regions in Sudan and Yemen, as well as in some Sudanese and Yemeni dialects, it may be either [gʲ] or [ʝ], representing the original pronunciation of Classical Arabic. Foreign words containing /g/ may be transcribed with ج, غ, ك, ق, گ, ڭ or ڨ, mainly depending on the regional spoken variety of Arabic or the commonly diacriticized Arabic letter. Note also that in northern Egypt, where the Arabic letter *jīm* (ج) is normally pronounced [g], a separate phoneme /ʒ/, which may be transcribed with چ, occurs in a small number of mostly non-Arabic loanwords, e.g., /ʒakitta/ 'jacket'.

/θ/ (ث) can be pronounced as [t] or even [s]. In some places of Maghreb it can be also pronounced as [t͡s].

/x/ and /ɣ/ (خ, غ) are velar, post-velar, or uvular.[61]

In many varieties, /ħ, ʕ/ (ح, ع) are actually <u>epiglottal</u> [ʜ, ʕ] (despite what is reported in many earlier works).

/l/ is pronounced as velarized [ɫ] in الله /ʔalla:h/, the name of God, q.e. Allah, when the word follows *a*, *ā*, *u* or *ū* (after *i* or *ī* it is unvelarized: بسـم الله *bismi l-lāh* /bismilla:h/). Some speakers velarize other occurrences of /l/ in MSA, in imitation of their spoken dialects.

The emphatic consonant /dˤ/ was actually pronounced [ɮˤ], or possibly [d͡ɮˤ][63] — either way, a highly unusual sound. The medieval Arabs actually termed their language *lughat al-ḍād* 'the language of the <u>D</u>ād' (the name of the letter used for this sound), since they thought the sound was unique to their language. (In fact, it also exists in a few other minority Semitic languages, e.g., Mehri.)

Arabic has consonants traditionally termed "emphatic" /tˤ, dˤ, sˤ, ðˤ/ (ط, ض, ص, ظ), which exhibit simultaneous <u>pharyngealization</u> [tˤ, dˤ, sˤ, ðˤ] as well as varying degrees of <u>velarization</u> [tˠ, dˠ, sˠ, ðˠ], so they may be written with the "Velarized or pharyngealized" diacritic (~) as: /t̰, d̰, s̰, ð̰/. This simultaneous articulation is described as "Retracted Tongue Root" by phonologists.[64] In some transcription systems, emphasis is shown by capitalizing the letter, for example, /dˤ/ is written ⟨D⟩; in others the letter is underlined or has a dot below it, for example, ⟨ḍ⟩.

Vowels and consonants can be phonologically short or long. Long (geminate) consonants are normally written doubled in Latin transcription (i.e. bb, dd, etc.), reflecting the presence of the Arabic diacritic mark *shaddah*, which indicates doubled consonants. In actual pronunciation, doubled consonants are held twice as long as short consonants. This consonant lengthening is phonemically contrastive: قبـل *qabala* 'he accepted' vs. قبّل *qabbala* 'he kissed'.

Syllable Structure

Arabic has two kinds of syllables: open syllables (CV) and (CVV) — and closed syllables (CVC), (CVVC) and (CVCC). The syllable types with two <u>morae</u> (units of time), i.e. CVC and CVV, are termed *heavy syllables*, while those with three morae, i.e. CVVC and CVCC, are *superheavy syllables*. Superheavy syllables in Classical Arabic occur in only two places: at the end of the sentence (due to <u>pausal</u> pronunciation) and in words such as حارّ *ḥārr* 'hot', مادّة *māddah* 'stuff, substance', تحــاجوا *taḥājjū* 'they disputed with each other', where a long *ā* occurs before two identical consonants (a former short vowel between the consonants has been lost). (In less formal pronunciations of Modern Standard Arabic, superheavy syllables are common at the end of words or before <u>clitic</u> suffixes such as *-nā* 'us, our', due to the deletion of final short vowels.)

In surface pronunciation, every vowel must be preceded by a consonant (which may include the <u>glottal stop</u> [ʔ]). There are no cases of <u>hiatus</u> within a word (where two vowels occur next to each other, without an intervening consonant). Some words do have an underlying vowel at the beginning, such as the definite article *al-* or words such as اشــترا *ishtarā* 'he bought', اجتمــاع *ijtimā'* 'meeting'. When actually pronounced, one of three things happens:

If the word occurs after another word ending in a consonant, there is a smooth transition from final consonant to initial vowel, e.g., اجتمــاع *al-ijtimā'* 'meeting' /alidʒtimaːʕ/.

If the word occurs after another word ending in a vowel, the initial vowel of the word is <u>elided</u>, e.g., المــدير بيـت *baytu (a)l-mudīr* 'house of the director' /bajtulmudiːr/.

If the word occurs at the beginning of an utterance, a glottal stop [ʔ] is added onto the beginning, e.g., البيـــت هو *al-baytu huwa* ... 'The house is ...' /ʔalbajtuhuwa ... /.

Stress

Word stress is not phonemically contrastive in Standard Arabic. It bears a strong relationship to vowel length. The basic rules for Modern Standard Arabic are:

A final vowel, long or short, may not be stressed.

Only one of the last three syllables may be stressed.

Given this restriction, the last heavy syllable (containing a long vowel or ending in a consonant) is stressed, if it is not the final syllable.

If the final syllable is super heavy and closed (of the form CVVC or CVCC) it receives stress.

If no syllable is heavy or super heavy, the first possible syllable (i.e. third from end) is stressed.

As a special exception, in Form VII and VIII verb forms stress may not be on the first syllable, despite the above rules: Hence *inkatab(a)* 'he subscribed' (whether or not the final short vowel is pronounced), *yankatib(u)* 'he subscribes' (whether or not the final short vowel is pronounced), *yankatib* 'he should subscribe (juss.)'. Likewise Form VIII *ishtarā* 'he bought', *yashtarī* 'he buys'.

Examples:*kitāb(un)* 'book', *kā-ti-b(un)* 'writer', *mak-ta-b(un)* 'desk', *ma-kā-ti-b(u)* 'desks', *mak-ta-ba-tun* 'library' (but *mak-ta-ba(-tun)* 'library' in short pronunciation), *ka-ta-bū* (Modern Standard Arabic) 'they wrote' = *ka-ta-bu* (dialect), *ka-ta-bū-h(u)* (Modern Standard Arabic) 'they wrote it' = *ka-ta-bū* (dialect), *ka-ta-ba-tā* (Modern Standard Arabic) 'they (dual, fem) wrote', *ka-*

tab-tu (Modern Standard Arabic) 'I wrote' = _ka-tabt_ (short form or dialect). Doubled consonants count as two consonants: _ma-jal-la-(tan)_ 'magazine', _ma-hall(-un)_ "place".

These rules may result in differently stressed syllables when final case endings are pronounced, vs. the normal situation where they are not pronounced, as in the above example of _mak-ta-ba-tun_ 'library' in full pronunciation, but _mak-ta-ba(-tun)_ 'library' in short pronunciation.

The restriction on final long vowels does not apply to the spoken dialects, where original final long vowels have been shortened and secondary final long vowels have arisen from loss of original final _-hu/hi_.

Some dialects have different stress rules. In the Cairo (Egyptian Arabic) dialect a heavy syllable may not carry stress more than two syllables from the end of a word, hence _mad-ra-sah_ 'school', _qā-hi-rah_ 'Cairo'. This also affects the way that Modern Standard Arabic is pronounced in Egypt. In the Arabic of Sanaa, stress is often retracted: _bay-tayn_ 'two houses', _mā-sat-hum_ 'their table', _ma-kā-tīb_ 'desks', _zā-rat-hīn_ 'sometimes', _mad-ra-sat-hum_ 'their school'. (In this dialect, only syllables with long vowels or diphthongs are considered heavy; in a two-syllable word, the final syllable can be stressed only if the preceding syllable is light; and in longer words, the final syllable cannot be stressed.)

Levels of pronunciation

The final short vowels (e.g., the case endings *-a -i -u* and mood endings *-u -a*) are often not pronounced in this language, despite forming part of the formal paradigm of nouns and verbs. The following levels of pronunciation exist:

Full Pronunciation with Pausa

This is the most formal level actually used in speech. All endings are pronounced as written, except at the end of an utterance, where the following changes occur:

Final short vowels are not pronounced. (But possibly an exception is made for feminine plural *-na* and shortened vowels in the jussive/imperative of defective verbs, e.g., *irmi!* 'throw!'".)

The entire indefinite noun endings *-in* and *-un* (with nunation) are left off. The ending *-an* is left off of nouns preceded by a *tā' marbūṭah* ة (i.e. the *-t* in the ending *-at-* that typically marks feminine nouns), but pronounced as *-ā* in other nouns (hence its writing in this fashion in the Arabic script).

The *tā' marbūṭah* itself (typically of feminine nouns) is pronounced as *h*. (At least, this is the case in extremely formal pronunciation, e.g., some Quranic recitations. In practice, this *h* is usually omitted.)

Formal Short Pronunciation

This is a formal level of pronunciation sometimes seen. It is somewhat like pronouncing all words as if they were in pausal position (with influence from the colloquial varieties). The following changes occur:

Most final short vowels are not pronounced. However, the following short vowels *are* pronounced:

feminine plural -*na*

shortened vowels in the jussive/imperative of defective verbs, e.g., *irmi!* 'throw!'

second-person singular feminine past-tense -*ti* and likewise *anti* 'you (fem. sg.)'

sometimes, first-person singular past-tense -*tu*

sometimes, second-person masculine past-tense -*ta* and likewise *anta* 'you (masc. sg.)'

final -*a* in certain short words, e.g., *laysa* 'is not', *sawfa* (future-tense marker)

The nunation endings -*an* -*in* -*un* are not pronounced. However, they *are* pronounced in adverbial accusative formations, e.g., *taqrīban* تَقْرِيبًا 'almost, approximately', *'ādatan* عَادَةً 'usually'.

The *tā' marbūṭah* ending ة is unpronounced, *except* in construct state nouns, where it sounds as *t* (and in adverbial accusative constructions, e.g., *'ādatan* عَادَةً 'usually', where the entire -*tan* is pronounced).

The masculine singular <u>nisbah</u> ending -*iyy* is actually pronounced -*ī* and is unstressed (but plural and feminine

singular forms, i.e. when followed by a suffix, still sound as -
iyy-).

Full endings (including case endings) occur when a <u>clitic</u>
object or possessive suffix is added (e.g., -*nā* 'us/our').

Informal Short Pronunciation

This is the pronunciation used by speakers of Modern
Standard Arabic in extemporaneous speech, i.e. when
producing new sentences rather than simply reading a
prepared text. It is similar to formal short pronunciation except
that the rules for dropping final vowels apply *even* when a clitic
suffix is added. Basically, short-vowel case and mood endings
are never pronounced and certain other changes occur that
echo the corresponding colloquial pronunciations. Specifically:

All the rules for formal short pronunciation apply, except
as follows.

The past tense singular endings written formally as -*tu* -*ta* -
ti are pronounced -*t* -*t* -*ti*. But masculine *'anta* is pronounced in
full.

Unlike in formal short pronunciation, the rules for
dropping or modifying final endings are also applied when a
<u>clitic</u> object or possessive suffix is added (e.g., -*nā* 'us/our'). If
this produces a sequence of three consonants, then one of the
following happens, depending on the speaker's native
colloquial variety:

A short vowel (e.g., -*i*- or -*ə*-) is consistently added, either
between the second and third or the first and second
consonants.

Or, a short vowel is added only if an otherwise unpronounceable sequence occurs, typically due to a violation of the sonority hierarchy (e.g., -rtn- is pronounced as a three-consonant cluster, but -trn- needs to be broken up).

Or, a short vowel is never added, but consonants like *r l m n* occurring between two other consonants will be pronounced as a syllabic consonant (as in the English words "butter bottle bottom button").

When a doubled consonant occurs before another consonant (or finally), it is often shortened to a single consonant rather than a vowel added. (But note that Moroccan Arabic never shortens doubled consonants or inserts short vowels to break up clusters, instead tolerating arbitrary-length series of arbitrary consonants and hence Moroccan Arabic speakers are likely to follow the same rules in their pronunciation of Modern Standard Arabic.)

The clitic suffixes themselves tend also to be changed, in a way that avoids many possible occurrences of three-consonant clusters. In particular, *-ka -ki -hu* generally sound as *-ak -ik -uh*.

Final long vowels are often shortened, merging with any short vowels that remain.

Depending on the level of formality, the speaker's education level, etc., various grammatical changes may occur in ways that echo the colloquial variants:

Any remaining case endings (e.g. masculine plural nominative *-ūn* vs. oblique *-īn*) will be leveled, with the oblique form used everywhere. (However, in words like *ab* 'father' and *akh* 'brother' with speciagl long-vowel case endings in the construct state, the nominative is used everywhere, hence *abū* 'father of', *akhū* 'brother of'.)

Feminine plural endings in verbs and clitic suffixes will often drop out, with the masculine plural endings used instead. If the speaker's native variety has feminine plural endings, they may be preserved, but will often be modified in the direction of the forms used in the speaker's native variety, e.g. *-an* instead of *-na*.

Dual endings will often drop out except on nouns and then used only for emphasis (similar to their use in the colloquial varieties); elsewhere, the plural endings are used (or feminine singular, if appropriate).

Greetings

تحيات

Hello!	مرحبا!	marHaba!
Good morning!	صباح الخير!	SabaaH al- khayr!
Good day!	يوم جيد!	yawm saxiid!
Good evening!	مساء الخير!	masaa' al- khayr!
How are you?	كيف حالك؟	kayfa Haaluka? (m.) (kayfa Haaluki? (f.))
Fine.	غرامة.	bikhayr.
Very well.	ممتاز.	jayyid jiddan.
So-so.	تقريبا.	la ba's.
What's your name?	ما اسمك؟	ma 'ismuk?
My name is...	اسمي هو ...	'ismii...
It's nice to meet you.	من اللطيف مقابلتك.	saxiidun bi liqaa'ika.
Goodbye.	وداعا.	maxa s- salaama.
See you soon.	اراك قريبا.	'araaka qariiban.
Goodnight.	تصبح على خير.	tiSbaH xala khayr.
Where do you live?	أين تعيش؟	'ayna taqTun?/'ayna taxiish?
I live in Beirut.	أنا أعيش في بيروت.	'axiishu fi Beirut.
This is my friend.	هذا صديقي.	haadha Sadiiqi.
This is my boyfriend.	هذا هو صديقي.	haadha SaaHibi.
This is my girlfriend.	هذا هو صديقتي.	haadhihi SaaHibati.
This is my husband.	هذا زوجي.	haadha zawji.
This is my wife.	هذه زوجتي.	haadhihi zawjati.
Please visit me!	يرجى زيارة لي!	'arju 'an tazuurani! (m.)/'arju 'an

		tazuuriini! (f.)
I had a wonderful time.	كان وقتا رائعا.	laqad 'amDaytu waqtan jamiilan.

Basic Phrases

الأساسـية العبــارات aleibarat al'asasia

Thank you.	.أ	shukran.
Thank you very much.	شكرا جزيلا.	shukran jaziilan.
You're welcome.	على الرحب و السعة.	'ahlan wa sahlan.
Please.	من فضلك.	rajaa'an.
Yes.	نعم فعلا.	'ajal./naxam.
No.	لا.	kalla./laa.
Excuse me.	عفوا.	xafwan.
Pardon me.	اعذرني.	xafwan./xuzran.
I'm sorry.	أنا آسف.	'anaa 'aasif.
I don't understand.	أنا لا أفهم.	la 'afham.
I don't speak Arabic.	أنا لا أتكلم العربية.	anaa la 'atakallam al-xarabiyya.
I don't speak Arabic very well.	أنا لا أتكلم العربية بشكل جيد للغاية.	'anaa laa 'atakallam al-xarabiyya jayyidan.
Do you speak English?	هل تتحدث الانجليزية؟	hal tatakallam 'ingilizi?
Speak slowly, please.	تحدث ببطء من فضلك.	rajaa'an takallam bi biT'.
Repeat, please.	أعد من فضلك.	'axid, min faDlak.
What's your name?	ما اسمك؟	ma 'ismuk?
How are you?	كيف حالك؟	kayfa Haaluka? (m.) (kayfa Haaluki? (f.))
Do you speak English?	هل تتحدث الانجليزية؟	hal tatakallam 'ingilizi?
Where is the subway?	أين هو مترو الانفاق؟	'ayna metro al-'anfaaq?
Where is a good restaurant?	أين هو مطعم جيد؟	hal hunaaka maTxamun jayyidun?

Is the tip included?	أيتضمن البقشيش؟	hal al-baqshiish maHsuub?
How much does that cost?	كم يكلف هذا ؟	kam huwa th- thaman?
Is there a public phone here?	هل هناك هاتف عمومي هنا؟	hal hunaaka haatifun 'umuumiyyun huna?
Can I get on the internet?	هل يمكنني الحصول على شبكة الانترنت؟	hal 'astaTiixa 'an 'astaxmil al-'internet?
Can you help me?	هل بإمكانك مساعدتي؟	hal tastaTiixa 'an tusaaxidani?

Animals

الحيوانات **alhayawanat**

bird	طائر	tayir
butterfly	فراشة	farashatan
cat	قط	qat
cow	بقرة	baqara
dog	الكلب	alkalb
donkey	الحمار	alhimar
duck	بطة	bitt
eagle	نسر	nusar
elephant	فيل	fil
frog	ضفدع	dafdae
giraffe	زرافة	zarafa
goose	أوز	'uwz
gorilla	غوريلا	ghurila
horse	حصان	hisan
lion	أسد	'asad

monkey	قرد	qarrad
mouse	فأر	fa'ar
parrot	ببغاء	babigha'
pig	خنزير	khinzir
scorpion	برج العقرب	burj aleaqarb
sheep	خروف	khuruf
snake	ثعبان	thueban
turtle	سلحفاة	silihafa
zebra	الحمار الوحشي	alhimar alwahshi

Transportation

وسائل النقل   wasayil alnnaql

bicycle	دراجه هوائية	dirajuh hawayiya
boat	قارب	qarib
bus	حافلة	hafila
car	سيارة	sayara
drive	يقود	yaqud
gasoline	الغازولين	alghazulin
road	طريق	tariq
ship	سفينة	safina
sign	إشارة	'iisharatan
stop	توقف	tawaqquf
tire	إطار العجلة	'iitar aleajala
train	قطار	qitar
transportation	وسائل النقل	wasayil alnnaql
truck	شاحنة	shahina

Places

موقـع   mawqie

beach	شاطئ	shati
church	كنيسة	kanisa
city	مدينة	madina
country	بلد	balad
farm	مزرعة	mazraea
hotel	الفندق	alfunduq
library	مكتبة	maktaba
location	موقع	mawqie
map	رسم خريطة	rusim kharita
market	سوق	suq
office	مكتب	maktab
park	منتزه	muntazzuh
prison	السجن	alssijn
restaurant	مطعم	mateam
school	مدرسة	madrasa
station	محطة	mahatt
street	شارع	sharie
theater	مسرح	masrah
town	بلدة	balda
university	جامعة	jamiea

Clothing

ملابــس   malabis

belt	حزام	hizam
blouse	بلوزة	bilawza
boot	حذاء	hidha'
cap	قبعة	qabea
coat	معطف	muetaf
dress	فستان	fastan
gloves	قفازات	qafazat
hat	قبعة	qabea
jacket	معطف	muetaf
jeans	جينز	jinz
pants	بنطال	bintal
shirt	قميص	qamis
shoe	حذاء	hidha'
skirt	تنورة	tanura
suit	بدلة	badla
T-shirt	تي شيرت	ty shayrt
wear	ارتداء	airtida'

Colors

اللـــون   alllawn

black	أسود	'asud
blue	أزرق	'azraq
brown	بنى	banaa
clear	واضح	wadh
cream	كريم	karim
dark	ظلام	zalam
gold	ذهب	dhahab
gray	رمادي	rmady
green	أخضر	'akhdir
pink	وردي	waradi
red	أحمر	'ahmar
white	أبيض	'abyad

People

الـناس   alnnas

adult	بالغ	baligh
boy	صبي	sabbi
child	طفل	tifl
girl	فتاة	fatatan
king	ملك	malik
neighbor	جار	jar
priest	كاهن	kahin
queen	ملكة	malika
teacher	مدرس	mudarris

Jobs

وظيفــة   wazifa

actor	الممثل	almumaththil
actress	ممثلة	mumaththila
architect	الهندسه المعماريه	alhandasuh almiemariuh
baker	خباز	khibaz
dancer	راقصة	raqisa
lawyer	محام	muham
police	شرطة	shurta
president	رئيس	rayiys
reporter	صحافي	sahafi
secretary	سكرتير	sikritir
soldier	جندي	jundi
student	طالب علم	talab eilm
waiter	نادل	nadil
work	عمل	eamal

Society

المجتمـــع almujtamae

ballot	تصويت	taswit
candidate	مرشح	murashshah
democracy	ديمقراطية	dimuqratia
election	انتخاب	aintikhab
mayor	عمدة	eumda
play	لعب	laeib
vote	تصويت	taswit
war	حرب	harb

Art

فــن fan

abstract	ملخص	mulakhkhas
art	فن	fan
artist	فنان	fannan
easel	حامل لقماشة الرسام	hamil liqamashat alrrssam
gallery	صالة عرض	salat earad
master	رئيسي	rayiysi
portrait	صورة	sura

Drinks

شـرب shurb

alcohol	كحول	kahul
beer	بيرة	bayratan
coffee	قهوة	qahuww
drinks	شرب	shurb
juice	عصير	easir
milk	حليب	halib
tea	شاي	shay
water	ماء	ma'an
whiskey	ويسكي	wayaski
wine	خمر	khamr

Food

طعام   taeam

Where is a good restaurant?	هل هناك مطعم جيد؟	hal hunaaka maTxamun jayyidun?
A table for two, please.	جدول لمدة سنتين، من فضلك.	Taawila li 'ithnayn, rajaa'an.
The menu, please.	القائمة، من فضلك.	qaa'imat Taxaam, rajaa'an.
The wine list, please.	قائمة النبيذ، من فضلك.	qaa'imat al- nabiidh, rajaa'an.
appetizers	مقبلات	mushahiyaat
main course	الطبق الرئيسي	al-Tabaq al-'asaasi
I would like something to drink.	أود أن تشرب شيئا.	'uridu mashruuban.
A glass of water, please.	كأسا من الماء من فضلك.	kubbaayat maa', rajaa'an.
A cup of tea, please.	كوب من الشاي، من فضلك.	kuub shaay, rajaa'an.
coffee with milk	قهوة مع الحليب	qahwatun maxa l- Haliib
Do you have a vegetarian dish?	هل لديك طبق نباتي؟	hal xindakum Tabaqun nabaatiyyun?
That's all.	هذا كل شيئ.	haadha kull shay'.
The check, please.	الحساب من فضلك.	al-faatuura, rajaa'an.
Is the tip included?	أيتضمن البقشيش؟	hal al-baqshiish maHsuub?
breakfast	وجبة فطور	al-fiTaar
Enjoy the meal!	استمتع بالوجبة!	'istamtix biTaxaamak! (m.)/'istamtixii biTaxaamik! (f.)
To your health!	لصحتك!	fi SiHatak! (m.)/fi SiHatik! (f.)
It's delicious!	أنه لذيذ!	'innahu ladhiidh! (m.)/'innaha ladhiidha! (f.)
a bottle of wine	زجاجة نبيذ	zujaajat nabiidh

I like my steak rare.	أنا أحب شريحة لحم بلدي نادرة.	'uriidu shariiHat laHm ghayr naaDija.
I like my steak medium.	أحب بلدي المتوسطة شريحة لحم.	'uriidu shariiHat laHm naaDijatun qaliilan.
I like my steak well done.	أحب بلدي شريحة لحم أحسنت.	'uriidu shariiHat laHm naDija jayyidan.
Another, please.	آخر، من فضلك.	waaHidun 'aakhar, rajaa'an. (m.) (waaHidatun 'ukhra, rajaa'an. (f.))
More, please.	أكثر من فضلك.	al maziid, rajaa'an.
Please pass the…	الرجاء تمرير …	rajaa'an marrir li l- …

apple	تفاحة	tafaha
banana	موز	muz
beef	لحم بقري	lahm baqari
bread	خبز	khabaz
breakfast	وجبة فطور	wajubbat futur
butter	زبدة	zabda
cake	كيكة	kayka
cheese	جبن	jubban
chicken	دجاج	dujaj
corn	حبوب ذرة	habub dharr
dinner	عشاء	easha'
eat	أكل	'akl

egg	بيضة	baydatan
fish	سمك	sammak
food	طعام	taeam
fork	شوكة	shawakk
ice	جليد	jalid
knife	سكين	sikin
lemon	ليمون	laymun
lunch	غداء	ghada'
orange	البرتقالي	alburtuqali
plate	طبق	tabaq
pork	لحم خنزير	lahm khinzir
rice	أرز	'arz
salt	ملح	milh
silver	فضي	fadi
soup	حساء	hasa'
spoon	ملعقة	maleaqa
sugar	السكر	alsskkar

Home

الرئيسـية الصــفحة alssafhat alrrayiysia

bedroom	غرفة نوم	ghurfat nawm
ceiling	سقف	saqf
chair	كرسي	kursi
door	باب	bab
garden	حديقة	hadiqa
home	الصفحة الرئيسية	alssafhat alrrayiysia
house	منزل	manzil
inside	في داخل	fi dakhil
key	مفتاح	miftah
kitchen	مطبخ	mutbakh
lamp	مصباح	misbah
lock	قفل	qafl
outside	في الخارج	fi alkharij
roof	سقف	saqf
room	غرفة	ghurfa
table	الطاولة	alttawila
toilet	مرحاض	mirhad
window	نافذة	nafidha
yard	حديقة منزل	hadiqat manzil

Electronics

ات إلكـــــتروني   'illiktruniat

camera	الة تصوير	alat taswir
computer	الحاسوب	alhasub
laptop	حاسوب محمول	hasub mahmul
phone	هاتف	hatif
radio	راديو	radiu
snow	ثلج	thalaj
telephone	هاتف	hatif
television	تلفزيون	tilfizyun

Nature

طبيعــــة   tabiea

dry	جاف	jaf
earth	أرض	'ard
forest	غابة	ghaba
ground	أرض	'ard
hill	تل	tal
hot	حار	harr
island	جزيرة	jazira
lake	بحيرة	buhayra
leaf	ورقة الشجر	waraqat alshshajar
moon	القمر	alqamar
mountain	جبل	jabal
ocean	محيط	mmuhit
plant	نبات	nabb'at
pool	حوض السباحة	hawd alssibaha
river	نهر	nahr
root	جذر	jidhr
sand	رمل	ramil
sea	بحر	bahr
seed	بذرة	bidharr
sky	سماء	sama'
soil	تربة	turba
space	الفضاء	alfada'
star	نجمة	najma

English / Arabic Phrasebook

stone	حجر	hijr
sun	شمس	shams
tree	شجرة	shajara
valley	الوادي	alwadi
wave	موجة	mawja
world	العالم	alealam

Measurements

قيــــاس   qias

centimeter	سنتيمتر	sanataymtr
inch	بوصة	busa
kilogram	كيلوغرام	kilughram
measurements	قياس	qias
meter	متر	mitr
pound	جنيه	junayh
square	مربع	murabbae
temperature	درجة الحرارة	darajat alharara
weight	وزن	wazn

Directions

الاتجاهـــات   alaittijahat

Where?	أين؟	'ayna?
Excuse me, where is...?	عفوا، أين هو ...؟	xafwan, 'ayna...?
Where are the taxis?	أين هي سيارات الأجرة؟	'ayna sayyarat al-'ujra?
Where is the bus?	اين الحافلة؟	'ayna l- baaS?
Where is the subway?	أين هو مترو الانفاق؟	'ayna metro al-'anfaaq?
Where is the exit?	اين المخرج؟	'ayna l- makhraj?
Is it near?	هو قرب؟	hal huwa qariib?
Is it far?	انه بعيد؟	hal huwa baxiid?
Go straight ahead.	الذهاب مباشرة إلى الأمام.	'idhhab 'ila l-'amaam.
Go that way.	السير في هذا الطريق.	idhhab min hazihi l- jiha.
Go back.	عُد	'irjax.
Turn right.	انعطف يمينا.	'inxatif yamiinan.
Turn left.	انعطف لليسار.	'inxatif yasaaran.
Take me to this address, please.	خذني إلى هذا العنوان من فضلك.	rajaa'an ila hadha al- xunwaan.
What is the fare?	ما هي أجرة؟	maa hiya l-'ughra?
Stop here, please.	توقف هنا من فضلك.	qif huna rajaa'an.
Does this bus go to Hamra street?	هل يذهب هذا الباص من شارع الحمرا؟	hal yazhab haadha l- baas 'ila shaarix al- Hamra'?
A map of the city, please.	خريطة للمدينة، من فضلك.	khaariTa lil- madiina, rajaa'an.
A subway map,	خريطة مترو الانفاق،	khaariTat al-metro, rajaa'an.

please.	من فضلك.	

Bottom	أسفل	'asfal
down	أسفل	'asfal
east	الشرق	alshrq
far	بعيدا	baeidanaan
left	اليسار	alyasar
low	منخفض	munkhafid
near	قرب	qurb
north	شمال	shamal
right	حق	haqq
side	جانب	janib
south	جنوب	janub
up	فوق	fawq
west	غرب	gharb

Seasons

الموسـم   almawsim

autumn	الخريف	alkharif
spring	ربيع	rbye
summer	الصيف	alssayf
winter	شتاء	shata'

Bath

حمام   hammam

bath mat	سجادة الحمام	sajadat alhamam
bath towel	منشفة الحمام	munshifat alhamam
bathe	استحم	aistaham
bathing suit	ثوب السباحة	thwb alssibaha
bathrobe	رداء الحمام	radda' alhamam
bathroom	حمام	hammam
bathtub	حوض الاستحمام	hawd alaistihmam
shower	دش	dash
soap	صابون	sabun
towel	منشفة	tawl

Numbers

أرقــام   'arqam

These numerals are those used when writing Arabic and are written from left to right. In Arabic they are known as "Indian numbers" (أرقام هندية / arqa-m hindiyyah). The term 'Arabic numerals' is also used to refer to 1, 2, 3, etc

.	١	٢	٣	٤	٥	٦	٧	٨	٩	١٠

صفر	واحد	إثنان	ثلاثة	أربعة	خمسة	ستة	سبعة	ثمانية	تسعة	عشرة
ṣifr	wāḥid	iṯnān	ṯalāṯah	'arba'ah	ḥamsah	sittah	sab'ah	ṯamāniyyah	tis'ah	'ašarah
0	1	2	3	4	5	6	7	8	9	10

zero	صفر	sifr
one	واحد	wahid
two	اثنان	athnan
three	ثلاثة	thlath
four	أربعة	arbe
five	خمسة	khms
six	ستة	st
seven	سبعة	sbe
eight	ثمانية	thmany
nine	تسعة	tse
ten	عشرة	eshr
eleven	أحد عشر	ahd eshr
twelve	اثني عشر	athnay eashar

thirteen	ثلاثة عشر	thlatht eshr
fourteen	أربعة عشرة	arbet eshr
fifteen	خمسة عشر	khmst eshr
sixteen	السادس عشر	alssadis eashar
seventeen	سبعة عشر	sbet eshr
eighteen	ثمانية عشرة	thmanyt eshr
nineteen	تسعة عشر	tiseat eashar
twenty	عشرون	eshrwn
twenty-one	واحد وعشرين	wahid weshryn
twenty-two	اثنين و عشرون	athnyn w eshrwn
twenty-three	ثلاث و عشرون	thlath w eshrwn
twenty-four	اربع وعشرون	arbe waeishrun
twenty-five	خمسة وعشرون	khmst waeishrun
twenty-six	ستة وعشرون	stt waeishrun
twenty-seven	سبعة وعشرين	sbet weshryn
twenty-eight	ثمانية وعشرون	thmanytan waeishrun
twenty-nine	تسعة و عشرون	tset w eshrwn
thirty	ثلاثون	thlathwn
forty	أربعون	'arbaeun
fifty	خمسون	khamsun
sixty	ستون	sutun
seventy	سبعون	sabeun
eighty	ثمانون	thamanun
ninety	تسعون	taseun
one hundred	مائة	miaya
one thousand	ألف	'alf
one thousand and	الف ل	'alf l

one		
billion	مليار	milyar
count	عد	eud
million	مليون	milyun
one hundred thousand	مئة الف	miat 'alf

Months

شـهر   shahr

date	تاريخ	tarikh
January	كانون الثاني	kanun alththani
February	فبراير	fibrayir
March	مارس	maris
April	أبريل	'abril
May	قد	qad
June	يونيو	yuniu
July	يوليو	yuliu
August	أغسطس	'aghustus
September	سبتمبر	sibtambar
October	شهر اكتوبر	shahr 'uktubar
November	تشرين الثاني	tishrin alththani
December	ديسمبر	disambir

Days

يـوم yawm

days	يوم	yawm
Sunday	الأحد	al'ahad
Monday	الإثنين	al'iithnin
Tuesday	الثلاثاء	alththulatha'
Wednesday	الأربعاء	al'arbiea'
Thursday	الخميس	alkhamis
Friday	الجمعة	aljumea
Saturday	يوم السبت	yawm alssabt
week	أسبوع	'usbue

Time

مرة marr

afternoon	بعد الظهر	baed alzzuhr
clock	ساعة حائط	saeatan hayit
evening	مساء	masa'
hour	ساعة	saea
minute	دقيقة	daqiqa
morning	صباح	sabah
night	ليل	layl
today	اليوم	alyawm
tomorrow	يوم غد	yawm ghad
year	عام	eam
yesterday	اليوم السابق	alyawm alssabiq

Body

الجسـم   aljism

arm	ذراع	dhirae
body	الجسم	aljism
bone	عظم	ezm
brain	دماغ	damagh
cheeks	الخدين	alkhadin
chest	صدر	sadar
chin	ذقن	dhaqan
elbow	كوع	kue
eye	عين	eayan
face	وجه	wajjah
fingers	أصابع	'asabie
foot	قدم	qadam
hair	شعر	shaear
hand	يد	yd
head	رئيس	rayiys
heart	قلب	qalb
knee	ركبة	rakba
leg	ساق	saq
neck	العنق	aleanq
nose	أنف	'anf
shoulder	كتف	kutuf
skin	بشرة	bashira
stomach	معدة	mueadd

sweat	عرق	earaq
teeth	اسنان	asnan
thigh	فخذ	fakhudh
throat	حلق	halq
thumb	إبهام اليد	'iibham alyad
toe	اصبع القدم	'iisbae alqadam
tooth	سن	sinn

Medical

دواء dawa'

blind	بليند	bilind
blood	دم	dam
dead	في ذمة الله تعالى	fi dhimmat alllah taealaa
deaf	أصم	'asm
drug	عقار	eiqqar
ear	إذن	'iidhan
healthy	صحي	sahi
hospital	مستشفى	mustashfaa
injury	جرح	jurh
kill	قتل	qutil
medicine	دواء	dawa'
pain	الم	'alam
patient	المريض	almarid
poison	سم	sm
sick	مريض	marid

Money

مال   mal

bank	بنك	bank
cheap	رخيص	rakhis
dollar	دولار	dular
money	مال	mal
price	السعر	alssier
sell	يبيع	yabie
store	متجر	matjar

Shopping

التســوق   alttasawwuq

How much does that cost?	كم هو الثمن؟	kam huwa th- thaman?
At what time does the store open?	في وقت ما لا فتح المحل؟	fii ayyi waqt yaftaHu l-maHall?
At what time does the store close?	في وقت ما لا يغلق المحل؟	fii ayyi waqt yaghliqu l-maHall?
What would you like?	ماذا تحب؟	maadha turiid?
Can I help you?	أيمكنني مساعدتك؟	hal lii 'an 'usaaxidak?
I would like this.	أود ذلك.	'uriidu haadha.
Here it is.	ها هو.	haa huwa. (m.) (haa hiya. (f.))
Is that all?	هل هذا كل شيء؟	hal haadha kullu shay'in?
I'd like to pay with cash.	أود أن الدفع نقدا.	'uriidu 'an 'adfaxa naqdan.
I'd like to pay by credit card.	أود أن الدفع بواسطة بطاقة الائتمان.	'uriidu 'an 'adfaxa bi biTaaqata l-'itimaan.
Can I order this online?	هل يمكنني طلب هذا على الانترنت؟	hal 'astaTiixa 'an aTlub haadha xala l-'internet?
Women's clothes	الملابس النسائية	malaabis nisaa'iyya
Men's clothes	ملابس رجالية	malaabis rijaaliyya
Blouse, skirt, dress	بلوزة، تنورة، فستان	bluuza, tannuura, fustaan
Pants, shirts, ties	والسراويل والقمصان، والعلاقات	banTaluun, qamiiS, ribaaT al-xunuq
Shoes and socks	الأحذية والجوارب	'aHzia wa jawariib
Jeans	جينز	jiinz
Bookstore	مكتبة لبيع الكتب	maHall al-kutub
Bakery	مخبز	makhbaz
Market	سوق	suuq
Supermarket	سوبر ماركت	suubermaarkit

Family

'أسـرة   usra

brother	شقيق	shaqiq
child	طفل	tifl
daughter	ابنة	aibna
family	أسرة	'usra
father	الآب	alab
female	أنثى	'unthaa
girl	فتاة	fatatan
grandfather	جد	jidd
grandmother	جدة	jidd
husband	زوج	zawj
male	ذكر	dhakar
man	رجل	rajul
marriage	زواج	zawaj
marry	تزوج	tazuj
mother	أم	'um
parent	أصل	asl
relationship	صلة	sila
sister	أخت	'ukht
son	ابن	abn
wedding	زفاف	zifaf
wife	زوجة	zawja
woman	امرأة	aimra'a

English / Arabic / Transliteration

الإنجليزية / العربية / الترجمة

al'iinjliziat / alearabiat / alttarjima

English	Arabic	Transliteration
abstract	ملخص	mulakhkhas
actor	الممثل	almumaththil
actress	ممثلة	mumaththila
adjectives	الصفات	alsfat
adult	بالغ	baligh
afternoon	بعد الظهر	baed alzzuhr
air	هواء	hawa'
airport	مطار	matar
alcohol	كحول	kahul
alcoholic drink	مشروب كحولي	mashrub khuly
alive	على قيد الحياة	ealaa qayd alhaya
Animals	الحيوانات	alhayawanat
apartment	شقة	shaqq
apple	تفاحة	tafaha
April	أبريل	'abril
architect	الهندسه المعماريه	alhandasuh almiemariuh
arm	ذراع	dhirae
army	جيش	jaysh
art	فن	fan

artist	فنان	fannan
attack	هجوم	hujum
August	أغسطس	'aghustus
author	مؤلف	muallaf
autumn	الخريف	alkharif
baby	طفل	tifl
back	الى الخلف	'ila alkhlf
back	الى الخلف	'ila alkhlf
bad	سيئة	sayiya
bag	حقيبة	haqiba
baker	خباز	khibaz
ball	كرة	kura
ballot	تصويت	taswit
banana	موز	muz
band	فرقة	firqa
bank	بنك	bank
bar	بار	bar
bath	حمام	hammam
bath mat	سجادة الحمام	sajadat alhamam
bath towel	منشفة الحمام	munshifat alhamam
bathe	استحم	aistaham
bathing suit	ثوب السباحة	thwb alssibaha
bathrobe	رداء الحمام	radda' alhamam
bathroom	حمام	hammam
bathroom	حمام	hammam
bathtub	حوض الاستحمام	hawd alaistihmam
beach	شاطئ	shati
beard	لحية	lahia

beat	تغلب	taghallab
beautiful	جميلة	jamila
bed	السرير	alssarir
bedroom	غرفة نوم	ghurfat nawm
beef	لحم بقري	lahm baqari
beer	بيرة	bayratan
belt	حزام	hizam
bend	ينحني	yanhani
bicycle	دراجه هوائية	dirajuh hawayiya
big	كبير	kabir
bill	فاتورة حساب	fatturat hisab
billion	مليار	milyar
bird	طائر	tayir
black	أسود	'asud
blind	بليند	bilind
blood	دم	dam
blouse	بلوزة	bilawza
blue	أزرق	'azraq
boat	قارب	qarib
body	الجسم	aljism
bone	عظم	ezm
book	كتاب	kitab
boot	حذاء	hidha'
bottle	زجاجة	zujaja
bottom	أسفل	'asfal
box	صندوق	sunduq
boy	صبي	sabbi
brain	دماغ	damagh

bread	خبز	khabaz
break	استراحة	aistiraha
breakfast	وجبة فطور	wajubbat futur
bridge	جسر	jisr
brother	شقيق	shaqiq
brown	بنى	banaa
build	بناء	bina'
building	بناء	bina'
burn	حرق	harq
bus	حافلة	hafila
butter	زبدة	zabda
butterfly	فراشة	farashatan
buy	يشترى	yushtaraa
buy	يشترى	yushtaraa
by	بواسطة	bwast
cake	كيكة	kayka
call	مكالمة	mukalima
camera	الة تصوير	alat taswir
camp	مخيم	mukhayam
candidate	مرشح	murashshah
cap	قبعة	qabea
car	سيارة	sayara
card	بطاقة	bitaqa
carry	حمل	hammal
cat	قط	qat
catch	قبض على	qubid ealaa
ceiling	سقف	saqf
cell	زنزانة	zinzana

centimeter	سنتيمتر	sanataymtr
chair	كرسي	kursi
cheap	رخيص	rakhis
cheeks	الخدين	alkhadin
cheese	جبن	jubban
chest	صدر	sadar
chicken	دجاج	dujaj
child	طفل	tifl
child	طفل	tifl
chin	ذقن	dhaqan
church	كنيسة	kanisa
circle	دائرة	dayira
city	مدينة	madina
clay	طين	tin
clean	نظيف	nazif
clear	واضح	wadh
clock	ساعة حائط	saeatan hayit
close	أغلق	'ughliq
clothing	ملابس	malabis
club	النادي	alnnadi
coat	معطف	muetaf
coffee	قهوة	qahuww
cold	برد	bard
color	اللون	alllawn
computer	الحاسوب	alhasub
consonant	حرف ساكن	harf sakin
contract	عقد	eaqad
cook	طبخ	tabbakh

English	عربي	
cool	بارد	barid
copper	نحاس	nahas
corn	حبوب ذرة	habub dharr
corner	ركن	rukn
count	عد	eud
country	بلد	balad
court	محكمة	mahkama
cow	بقرة	baqara
cream	كريم	karim
crowd	حشد	hashd
cry	بكاء bika'	
cup	كوب	kub
curved	منحن	munhun
cut	قطع	qate
dance	رقص	raqus
dancer	راقصة	raqisa
dark	ظلام	zalam
date	تاريخ	tarikh
daughter	ابنة	aibna
days	يوم	yawm
dead	في ذمة الله تعالى	fi dhimmat alllah taealaa
deaf	أصم	'asm
death	الموت	almawt
December	ديسمبر	disambir
deep	عميق	eamiq
democracy	ديمقراطية	dimuqratia
diamond	الماس	almas
dictionary	قاموس	qamus

die	مات	mat
dig	حفر	hafr
dinner	عشاء	easha'
Directions	الاتجاهات	alaittijahat
Directions	الاتجاهات	alaittijahat
dirty	قذر	qadhar
disease	مرض	marad
doctor	طبيب	tabib
dog	الكلب	alkalb
dollar	دولار	dular
donkey	الحمار	alhimar
door	باب	bab
dot	نقطة	nuqta
down	أسفل	'asfal
draw	رسم	rusim
dream	حلم	hulm
dress	فستان	fastan
drinks	شرب	shurb
drive	يقود	yaqud
drug	عقار	eiqqar
dry	جاف	jaf
duck	بطة	bitt
dust	غبار	ghabar
eagle	نسر	nusar
ear	إذن	'iidhan
earth	أرض	'ard
easel	حامل لقماشة الرسام	hamil liqamashat alrrssam

east	الشرق	alshrq
eat	أكل	'akl
edge	حافة	hafa
egg	بيضة	baydatan
eight	ثمانية	thmany
eighteen	ثمانية عشرة	thmanyt eshr
eighty	ثمانون	thamanun
elbow	كوع	kue
election	انتخاب	aintikhab
electronics	إلكترونيات	'illiktruniat
elephant	فيل	fil
eleven	أحد عشر	ahd eshr
energy	طاقة	taqa
engine	محرك	maharrak
engine	محرك	maharrak
evening	مساء	masa'
exercise	ممارسة	mumarasa
expensive	مكلفة	mukallafa
explode	تفجر	tafjur
eye	عين	eayan
face	وجه	wajjah
fall	خريف	kharif
family	أسرة	'usra
fan	مروحة	muruha
fan	مروحة	muruha
far	بعيدا	baeidanaan
farm	مزرعة	mazraea
fast	بسرعة	bsre

father	الآب	alab
February	فبراير	fibrayir
feed	تغذية	taghdhia
female	أنثى	'unthaa
fifteen	خمسة عشر	khmst eshr
fifty	خمسون	khamsun
fight	حارب	harab
find	تجد	tajid
finger	اصبع اليد	'iisbae alyad
fingers	أصابع	'asabie
fire	نار	nar
fish	سمك	sammak
five	خمسة	khms
flat	مسطحة	mustaha
floor	أرضية	'ardia
flower	زهرة	zahra
fly	يطير	yatir
follow	إتبع	'itbae
food	طعام	taeam
food	طعام	taeam
foot	قدم	qadam
forest	غابة	ghaba
fork	شوكة	shawakk
forty	أربعون	'arbaeun
four	أربعة	arbe
fourteen	أربعة عشرة	arbet eshr
Friday	الجمعة	aljumea
frog	ضفدع	dafdae

front	جبهة	jabha
gallery	صالة عرض	salat earad
game	لعبة	lueba
garden	حديقة	hadiqa
gasoline	الغازولين	alghazulin
gift	هدية	hadia
giraffe	زرافة	zarafa
girl	فتاة	fatatan
girl	فتاة	fatatan
glass	زجاج	zujaj
gloves	قفازات	qafazat
God	الله	alllah
gold	ذهب	dhahab
gold	ذهب	dhahab
good	جيد	jayid
good morning	صباح الخير	sabah alkhyr
goose	أوز	'uwz
gorilla	غوريلا	ghurila
grandfather	جد	jidd
grandmother	جدة	jidd
grass	عشب	eshb
gray	رمادي	rmady
green	أخضر	'akhdir
ground	أرض	'ard
grow	تنمو	tanmu
gun	بندقية	bunduqia
hair	شعر	shaear
half	نصف	nsf

hand	يد	yd
hang	علق	ealaq
happy	سعيد	saeid
hard	الصعب	alssaeb
hat	قبعة	qabea
he	هو	hu
head	رئيس	rayiys
healthy	صحي	sahi
hear	سمع	sumie
heart	قلب	qalb
heat	حرارة	harara
heaven	الجنة	aljann
heavy	ثقيل	thaqil
hell	الجحيم	aljahim
high	عالي	eali
hill	تل	tal
hole	ثقب	thaqab
home	الصفحة الرئيسية	alssafhat alrrayiysia
horse	حصان	hisan
hospital	مستشفى	mustashfaa
hot	حار	harr
hotel	الفندق	alfunduq
hour	ساعة	saea
house	منزل	manzil
husband	زوج	zawj
I	أنا	'ana
ice	جليد	jalid
iguana	الإغوانا	al'iighwana

image	صورة	sura
inch	بوصة	busa
injury	جرح	jurh
inside	في داخل	fi dakhil
instrument	صك	sak
island	جزيرة	jazira
island	جزيرة	jazira
it	هذا	hadha
jacket	معطف	muetaf
January	كانون الثاني	kanun alththani
jeans	جينز	jinz
job	وظيفة	wazifa
Jobs	وظيفة	wazifa
juice	عصير	easir
July	يوليو	yuliu
jump	قفز	qafaz
June	يونيو	yuniu
key	مفتاح	miftah
kill	قتل	qutil
kilogram	كيلوغرام	kilughram
king	ملك	malik
kiss	قبلة	qibla
kitchen	مطبخ	mutbakh
knee	ركبة	rakba
knife	سكين	sikin
lake	بحيرة	buhayra
lamp	مصباح	misbah
laptop	حاسوب محمول	hasub mahmul

laugh	ضحك	dahk
lawyer	محام	muham
leaf	ورقة الشجر	waraqat alshshajar
learn	تعلم	taeallam
left	اليسار	alyasar
leg	ساق	saq
lemon	ليمون	laymun
letter	خطاب	khitab
library	مكتبة	maktaba
lie down	أنسدح	'ansadih
lift	مصعد	museid
light	ضوء	daw'
lion	أسد	'asad
lip	شفة	shifa
location	موقع	mawqie
lock	قفل	qafl
long	طويل	tawil
loose	فضفاض	fadafad
lose	تخسر	takhsir
loud	عال	eal
love	حب	hubb
low	منخفض	munkhafid
lunch	غداء	ghada'
magazine	مجلة	majall
male	ذكر	dhakar
man	رجل	rajul
manager	مدير	mudir
map	رسم خريطة	rusim kharita

English	عربي	
March	مارس	maris
market	سوق	suq
marriage	زواج	zawaj
marry	تزوج	tazuj
master	رئيسي	rayiysi
material	مادة	madd
May	قد	qad
mayor	عمدة	eumda
mean	تعني	taeni
measurements	قياس	qias
medicine	دواء	dawa'
melt	صهر	sahr
metal	معدن	muedan
meter	متر	mitr
milk	حليب	halib
million	مليون	milyun
minute	دقيقة	daqiqa
miscellaneous	متفرقات	mutafarriqat
mix	مزج	mizj
mix	مزج	mizj
Monday	الإثنين	al'iithnin
money	مال	mal
monkey	قرد	qarrad
month	شهر	shahr
moon	القمر	alqamar
morning	صباح	sabah
mother	أم	'um
mountain	جبل	jabal

mouse	فأر	fa'ar
mouth	فم	fam
movie	فيلم	film
murder	قتل	qutil
music	موسيقى	musiqaa
musical	موسيقي	musiqi
narrow	ضيق	dayiq
nature	طبيعة	tabiea
near	قرب	qurb
neck	العنق	aleanq
needle	إبرة	'iibratan
neighbor	جار	jar
network	شبكة	shabaka
new	جديد	jadid
newspaper	جريدة	jarida
nice	لطيف	latif
night	ليل	layl
nine	تسعة	tse
nineteen	تسعة عشر	tiseat eashar
ninety	تسعون	taseun
no	لا	la
north	شمال	shamal
nose	أنف	'anf
note	ملاحظة	mulahaza
November	تشرين الثاني	tishrin alththani
nuclear	نووي	nawawi
numbers	أرقام	'arqam
ocean	محيط	mmuhit

English	العربية	Transliteration
October	شهر اكتوبر	shahr 'uktubar
office	مكتب	maktab
oil	نفط	nft
old	قديم	qadim
one	واحد	wahid
one hundred	مائة	miaya
one hundred thousand	مئة الف	miat 'alf
one thousand	ألف	'alf
one thousand and one	الف ل	'alf l
open	فتح	fath
orange	البرتقالي	alburtuqali
our	لنا	lana
outside	في الخارج	fi alkharij
page	صفحة	safha
pain	الم	'alam
paint	رسم	rusim
pants	بنطال	bintal
paper	ورقة	waraqatan
parent	أصل	asl
park	منتزه	muntazzuh
parrot	ببغاء	babigha'
pass	مرر	marrar
patient	المريض	almarid
pattern	نمط	namat
pay	دفع	dafe
peace	سلام	salam
pen	قلم جاف	qalam jaf

pencil	قلم	qalam
people	الناس	alnnas
person	شخص	shakhs
phone	هاتف	hatif
photograph	تصوير	taswir
piece	قطعة	qitea
pig	خنزير	khinzir
pink	وردي	waradi
plane	طائرة	tayira
plant	نبات	nabb'at
plastic	البلاستيك	albilastik
plate	طبق	tabaq
play	لعب	laeib
player	لاعب	laeib
pocket	جيب	jayb
poison	سم	sm
police	شرطة	shurta
pool	حوض السباحة	hawd alssibaha
poor	فقير	faqir
pork	لحم خنزير	lahm khinzir
portrait	صورة	sura
pound	جنيه	junayh
pray	صلى	salla
president	رئيس	rayiys
price	السعر	alssier
priest	كاهن	kahin
prison	السجن	alssijn
program	برنامج	barnamaj

pronoun	ضمير	damir
pull	سحب	sahb
push	إدفع	'iidfae
queen	ملكة	malika
quiet	هادئ	hadi
race	سباق	sibaq
race	سباق	sibaq
radio	راديو	radiu
rain	مطر	mtr
red	أحمر	'ahmar
relationship	صلة	sila
religion	دين	din
reporter	صحافي	sahafi
restaurant	مطعم	mateam
rice	أرز	'arz
rich	غني	ghani
right	حق	haqq
right	حق	haqq
ring	حلقة	halqa
river	نهر	nahr
road	طريق	tariq
roof	سقف	saqf
room	غرفة	ghurfa
root	جذر	jidhr
run	يجري	yajri
sad	حزين	hazin
salt	ملح	milh
sand	رمل	ramil

Saturday	يوم السبت	yawm alssabt
school	مدرسة	madrasa
science	علم	eulim
scorpion	برج العقرب	burj aleaqarb
screen	شاشة	shasha
sea	بحر	bahr
seasonal	موسمي	mawsimi
seasons	الموسم	almawsim
second	ثانيا	thaniaan
secretary	سكرتير	sikritir
see	يرى	yaraa
seed	بذرة	bidharr
sell	يبيع	yabie
September	سبتمبر	sibtambar
seven	سبعة	sbe
seventeen	سبعة عشر	sbet eshr
seventy	سبعون	sabeun
shake	هز	hazz
shallow	سطحية	satahia
she	هي	hi
sheep	خروف	khuruf
ship	سفينة	safina
shirt	قميص	qamis
shoe	حذاء	hidha'
shoot	أطلق النار	'atlaq alnnar
short	قصير	qasir
shoulder	كتف	kutuf
shower	دش	dash

English	عربي	
sick	مريض	marid
side	جانب	janib
sign	إشارة	'iisharatan
silver	فضي	fadi
sing	غنى	ghina
sister	أخت	'ukht
sit	جلس	jals
six	ستة	st
sixteen	السادس عشر	alssadis eashar
sixty	ستون	sutun
skin	بشرة	bashira
skirt	تنورة	tanura
sky	سماء	sama'
sleep	نوم	nawm
slow	بطيء	bati'
small	صغير	saghir
smell	رائحة	rayiha
smile	ابتسامة	aibtisama
snake	ثعبان	thueban
snow	ثلج	thalaj
soap	صابون	sabun
society	المجتمع	almujtamae
soft	ناعم	naeam
soil	تربة	turba
soldier	جندي	jundi
son	ابن	abn
song	أغنية	'aghnia
sound	صوت	sawt

English	Arabic	Transliteration
soup	حساء	hasa'
south	جنوب	janub
space	الفضاء	alfada'
speak	تحدث	tahduth
spoon	ملعقة	maleaqa
sport	رياضة	riada
spring	ربيع	rbye
spring	ربيع	rbye
square	مربع	murabbae
stain	وصمة	wasamm
stand	موقف	mwqf
star	نجمة	najma
station	محطة	mahatt
stomach	معدة	mueadd
stone	حجر	hijr
stop	توقف	tawaqquf
store	متجر	matjar
story	قصة	qiss
straight	مباشرة	mubashara
street	شارع	sharie
strong	قوي	qawi
student	طالب علم	talab eilm
sugar	السكر	alsskkar
suit	بدلة	badla
summer	الصيف	alssayf
sun	شمس	shams
Sunday	الأحد	al'ahad
sweat	عرق	earaq

English	العربية	Transliteration
swim	سباحة	sibaha
table	الطاولة	alttawila
tall	طويل	tawil
taste	طعم	taem
tea	شاي	shay
teach	علم	eulim
teacher	مدرس	mudarris
team	الفريق	alfariq
tear	تمزق	tamazzuq
technology	تكنولوجيا	taknulujia
teeth	اسنان	asnan
telephone	هاتف	hatif
television	تلفزيون	tilfizyun
temperature	درجة الحرارة	darajat alharara
ten	عشرة	eshr
theater	مسرح	masrah
Them	هم	hum
They	هم	hum
thick	سميك	samik
thigh	فخذ	fakhudh
thin	رقيق	raqiq
think	فكر في	fakkar fi
thirteen	ثلاثة عشر	thlatht eshr
thirty	ثلاثون	thlathwn
three	ثلاثة	thlath
throat	حلق	halq
throw	رمي	ramy
thumb	إبهام اليد	'iibham alyad

English	Arabic	Transliteration
Thursday	الخميس	alkhamis
ticket	تذكرة	tadhkira
tight	ضيق	dayiq
time	مرة	marr
tire	إطار العجلة	'iitar aleajala
today	اليوم	alyawm
toe	اصبع القدم	'iisbae alqadam
toilet	مرحاض	mirhad
tomorrow	يوم غد	yawm ghad
tongue	لسان	lisan
tool	أداة	'adatan
tooth	سن	sinn
top	أعلى	'aelaa
touch	لمس	lams
towel	منشفة	tawl
town	بلدة	balda
train	قطار	qitar
transportation	وسائل النقل	wasayil alnnaql
tree	شجرة	shajara
truck	شاحنة	shahina
T-shirt	تي شيرت	ty shayrt
Tuesday	الثلاثاء	alththulatha'
turn	منعطف	muneataf
turtle	سلحفاة	silihafa
twelve	اثني عشر	athnay eashar
twenty	عشرون	eshrwn
twenty-eight	ثمانية وعشرون	thmanytan waeishrun
twenty-five	خمسة وعشرون	khmst waeishrun

twenty-four	اربع وعشرون	arbe waeishrun
twenty-nine	تسعة و عشرون	tset w eshrwn
twenty-one	واحد وعشرين	wahid weshryn
twenty-seven	سبعة وعشرين	sbet weshryn
twenty-six	ستة وعشرون	stt waeishrun
twenty-three	ثلاث و عشرون	thlath w eshrwn
twenty-two	اثنين و عشرون	athnyn w eshrwn
two	اثنان	athnan
ugly	قبيح	qabih
university	جامعة	jamiea
up	فوق	fawq
up	فوق	fawq
valley	الوادي	alwadi
Verb	الفعل	alfiel
victim	ضحية	dahia
voice	صوت	sawt
vote	تصويت	taswit
vowel	حرف متحرك	harf mutaharrik
waiter	نادل	nadil
walk	سير	sayr
wall	جدار	jadar
war	حرب	harb
warm	دافئ	dafi
wash	غسل	ghasil
watch	راقب	raqib
water	ماء	ma'an
wave	موجة	mawja
we	نحن	nahn

weak	ضعيف	daeif
wear	ارتداء	airtida'
wedding	زفاف	zifaf
Wednesday	الأربعاء	al'arbiea'
week	أسبوع	'usbue
weight	وزن	wazn
west	غرب	gharb
wet	مبلل	mublil
whiskey	ويسكي	wayaski
white	أبيض	'abyad
wide	واسع	wasie
wife	زوجة	zawja
win	انتصر	antasar
wind	ريح	rih
window	نافذة	nafidha
wine	خمر	khamr
wing	جناح	junah
winter	شتاء	shata'
woman	امرأة	aimra'a
wood	خشب	khushub
work	عمل	eamal
world	العالم	alealam
write	اكتب	aktab
yard	حديقة منزل	hadiqat manzil
year	عام	eam
yellow	أصفر	'asfar
yes	نعم فعلا	nem fielaan
yesterday	اليوم السابق	alyawm alssabiq

you	أنت	'ant
young	شاب	shabb
zebra	الحمار الوحشي	alhimar alwahshi
zero	صفر	sifr

Arabic / English / Transliteration

/ العربية /الإنجليزية / الترجمة

alearabiat / al'iinjliziat / alttarjima

Arabic	English	Transliteration
ابتسامة	smile	aibtisama
ابن	son	abn
ابنة	daughter	aibna
اثنان	two	athnan
اثني عشر	twelve	athnay eashar
اثنين و عشرون	twenty-two	athnyn w eshrwn
اربع وعشرون	twenty-four	arbe waeishrun
ارتداء	wear	airtida'
استحم	bathe	aistaham
استراحة	break	aistiraha
اسنان	teeth	asnan
اصبع القدم	toe	'iisbae alqadam
اصبع اليد	finger	'iisbae alyad
اكتب	write	aktab
الاتجاهات	Directions	alaittijahat
الاتجاهات	Directions	alaittijahat
الإثنين	Monday	al'iithnin
الإغوانا	iguana	al'iighwana
الأحد	Sunday	al'ahad
الأربعاء	Wednesday	al'arbiea'
الآب	father	alab
البرتقالي	orange	alburtuqali
البلاستيك	plastic	albilastik
الة تصوير	camera	alat taswir
الثلاثاء	Tuesday	alththulatha'

الجحيم	hell	aljahim
الجسم	body	aljism
الجمعة	Friday	aljumea
الجنة	heaven	aljann
الحاسوب	computer	alhasub
الحمار	donkey	alhimar
الحمار الوحشي	zebra	alhimar alwahshi
الحيوانات	Animals	alhayawanat
الخدين	cheeks	alkhadin
الخريف	autumn	alkharif
الخميس	Thursday	alkhamis
السادس عشر	sixteen	alssadis eashar
السجن	prison	alssijn
السرير	bed	alssarir
السعر	price	alssier
السكر	sugar	alsskkar
الشرق	east	alshrq
الصعب	hard	alssaeb
الصفات	adjectives	alsfat alssafhat
الصفحة الرئيسية	home	alrrayiysia
الصيف	summer	alssayf
الطاولة	table	alttawila
العالم	world	alealam
العنق	neck	aleanq
الغازولين	gasoline	alghazulin
الف ل	one thousand and one	'alf l
الفريق	team	alfariq
الفضاء	space	alfada'
الفعل	Verb	alfiel
الفندق	hotel	alfunduq

القمر	moon	alqamar
الكلب	dog	alkalb
الله	God	alllah
اللون	color	alllawn
الم	pain	'alam
الماس	diamond	almas
المجتمع	society	almujtamae
المريض	patient	almarid
الممثل	actor	almumaththil
الموت	death	almawt
الموسم	seasons	almawsim
النادي	club	alnnadi
الناس	people	alnnas
		alhandasuh
الهندسه المعماريه	architect	almiemariuh
الوادي	valley	alwadi
الى الخلف	back	'ila alkhlf
الى الخلف	back	'ila alkhlf
اليسار	left	alyasar
اليوم	today	alyawm
اليوم السابق	yesterday	alyawm alssabiq
امرأة	woman	aimra'a
انتخاب	election	aintikhab
انتصر	win	antasar
إبرة	needle	'iibratan
إبهام اليد	thumb	'iibham alyad
إتبع	follow	'itbae
إدفع	push	'iidfae
إذن	ear	'iidhan
إشارة	sign	'iisharatan
إطار العجلة	tire	'iitar aleajala
إلكترونيات	electronics	'illiktruniat

أبريل	April	'abril
أبيض	white	'abyad
أحد عشر	eleven	ahd eshr
أحمر	red	'ahmar
أخت	sister	'ukht
أخضر	green	'akhdir
أداة	tool	'adatan
أربعة	four	arbe
أربعة عشرة	fourteen	arbet eshr
أربعون	forty	'arbaeun
أرز	rice	'arz
أرض	earth	'ard
أرض	ground	'ard
أرضية	floor	'ardia
أرقام	numbers	'arqam
أزرق	blue	'azraq
أسبوع	week	'usbue
أسد	lion	'asad
أسرة	family	'usra
أسفل	bottom	'asfal
أسفل	down	'asfal
أسود	black	'asud
أصابع	fingers	'asabie
أصفر	yellow	'asfar
أصل	parent	asl
أصم	deaf	'asm
أطلق النار	shoot	'atlaq alnnar
أعلى	top	'aelaa
أغسطس	August	'aghustus
أغلق	close	'ughliq
أغنية	song	'aghnia
أكل	eat	'akl

ألف	one thousand	'alf
أم	mother	'um
أنا	I	'ana
أنت	you	'ant
أنثى	female	'unthaa
أنسدح	lie down	'ansadih
أنف	nose	'anf
أوز	goose	'uwz
باب	door	bab
بار	bar	bar
بارد	cool	barid
بالغ	adult	baligh
بيغاء	parrot	babigha'
بحر	sea	bahr
بحيرة	lake	buhayra
بدلة	suit	badla
بذرة	seed	bidharr
برج العقرب	scorpion	burj aleaqarb
برد	cold	bard
برنامج	program	barnamaj
بسرعة	fast	bsre
بشرة	skin	bashira
بطاقة	card	bitaqa
بطة	duck	bitt
بطيء	slow	bati'
بعد الظهر	afternoon	baed alzzuhr
بعيدا	far	baeidanaan
بقرة	cow	baqara
بكاء	cry	bika'
بلد	country	balad
بلدة	town	balda
بلوزة	blouse	bilawza

بليند	blind	bilind
بناء	build	bina'
بناء	building	bina'
بندقية	gun	bunduqia
بنطال	pants	bintal
بنك	bank	bank
بنى	brown	banaa
بواسطة	by	bwast
بوصة	inch	busa
بيرة	beer	bayratan
بيضة	egg	baydatan
تاريخ	date	tarikh
تجد	find	tajid
تحدث	speak	tahduth
تخسر	lose	takhsir
تذكرة	ticket	tadhkira
تربة	soil	turba
تزوج	marry	tazuj
تسعة	nine	tse
تسعة عشر	nineteen	tiseat eashar
تسعة و عشرون	twenty-nine	tset w eshrwn
تسعون	ninety	taseun
تشرين الثاني	November	tishrin alththani
تصويت	ballot	taswit
تصويت	vote	taswit
تصوير	photograph	taswir
تعلم	learn	taeallam
تعني	mean	taeni
تغذية	feed	taghdhia
تغلب	beat	taghallab
تفاحة	apple	tafaha
تفجر	explode	tafjur

تكنولوجيا	technology	taknulujia
تل	hill	tal
تلفزيون	television	tilfizyun
تمزق	tear	tamazzuq
تنمو	grow	tanmu
تنورة	skirt	tanura
توقف	stop	tawaqquf
تي شيرت	T-shirt	ty shayrt
ثانيا	second	thaniaan
ثعبان	snake	thueban
ثقب	hole	thaqab
ثقيل	heavy	thaqil
ثلاث و عشرون	twenty-three	thlath w eshrwn
ثلاثة	three	thlath
ثلاثة عشر	thirteen	thlatht eshr
ثلاثون	thirty	thlathwn
ثلج	snow	thalaj
ثمانون	eighty	thamanun
ثمانية	eight	thmany
ثمانية عشرة	eighteen	thmanyt eshr
ثمانية وعشرون	twenty-eight	thmanytan waeishrun
ثوب السباحة	bathing suit	thwb alssibaha
جار	neighbor	jar
جاف	*dry*	jaf
جامعة	university	jamiea
جانب	side	janib
جبل	mountain	jabal
جبن	cheese	jubban
جبهة	front	jabha
جد	grandfather	jidd
جدار	wall	jadar

جدة	grandmother	jidd
جديد	new	jadid
جذر	root	jidhr
جرح	injury	jurh
جريدة	newspaper	jarida
جزيرة	island	jazira
جزيرة	island	jazira
جسر	bridge	jisr
جلس	sit	jals
جليد	ice	jalid
جميلة	beautiful	jamila
جناح	wing	junah
جندي	soldier	jundi
جنوب	south	janub
جنيه	pound	junayh
جيب	pocket	jayb
جيد	good	jayid
جيش	army	jaysh
جينز	jeans	jinz
حار	hot	harr
حارب	fight	harab
حاسوب محمول	laptop	hasub mahmul
حافة	edge	hafa
حافلة	bus	hafila
حامل لقماشة الرسام	easel	hamil liqamashat alrrssam
حب	love	hubb
حبوب ذرة	corn	habub dharr
حجر	stone	hijr
حديقة	garden	hadiqa
حديقة منزل	yard	hadiqat manzil
حذاء	boot	hidha'

حذاء	shoe	hidha'
حرارة	heat	harara
حرب	war	harb
حرف ساكن	consonant	harf sakin
حرف متحرك	vowel	harf mutaharrik
حرق	burn	harq
حزام	belt	hizam
حزين	sad	hazin
حساء	soup	hasa'
حشد	crowd	hashd
حصان	horse	hisan
حفر	dig	hafr
حق	right	haqq
حق	right	haqq
حقيبة	bag	haqiba
حلق	throat	halq
حلقة	ring	halqa
حلم	dream	hulm
حليب	milk	halib
حمام	bath	hammam
حمام	bathroom	hammam
حمام	bathroom	hammam
حمل	carry	hammal
حوض الاستحمام	bathtub	hawd alaistihmam
حوض السباحة	pool	hawd alssibaha
خباز	baker	khibaz
خبز	bread	khabaz
خروف	sheep	khuruf
خريف	fall	kharif
خشب	wood	khushub
خطاب	letter	khitab
خمر	wine	khamr

خمسة	five	khms
خمسة عشر	fifteen	khmst eshr
خمسة وعشرون	twenty-five	khmst waeishrun
خمسون	fifty	khamsun
خنزير	pig	khinzir
دافئ	warm	dafi
دائرة	circle	dayira
دجاج	chicken	dujaj
دراجه هوائية	bicycle	dirajuh hawayiya
درجة الحرارة	temperature	darajat alharara
دش	shower	dash
دفع	pay	dafe
دقيقة	minute	daqiqa
دم	blood	dam
دماغ	brain	damagh
دواء	medicine	dawa'
دولار	dollar	dular
ديسمبر	December	disambir
ديمقراطية	democracy	dimuqratia
دين	religion	din
ذراع	arm	dhirae
ذقن	chin	dhaqan
ذكر	male	dhakar
ذهب	gold	dhahab
ذهب	gold	dhahab
راديو	radio	radiu
راقب	watch	raqib
راقصة	dancer	raqisa
رائحة	smell	rayiha
ربيع	spring	rbye
ربيع	spring	rbye
رجل	man	rajul

رخيص	cheap	rakhis
رداء الحمام	bathrobe	radda' alhamam
رسم	draw	rusim
رسم	paint	rusim
رسم خريطة	map	rusim kharita
رقص	dance	raqus
رقيق	thin	raqiq
ركبة	knee	rakba
ركن	corner	rukn
رمادي	gray	rmady
رمل	sand	ramil
رمي	throw	ramy
رياضة	sport	riada
ريح	wind	rih
رئيس	head	rayiys
رئيس	president	rayiys
رئيسي	master	rayiysi
زبدة	butter	zabda
زجاج	glass	zujaj
زجاجة	bottle	zujaja
زرافة	giraffe	zarafa
زفاف	wedding	zifaf
زنزانة	cell	zinzana
زهرة	flower	zahra
زواج	marriage	zawaj
زوج	husband	zawj
زوجة	wife	zawja
ساعة	hour	saea
ساعة حائط	clock	saeatan hayit
ساق	leg	saq
سباحة	swim	sibaha
سباق	race	sibaq

سباق	race	sibaq
سبتمبر	September	sibtambar
سبعة	seven	sbe
سبعة عشر	seventeen	sbet eshr
سبعة وعشرين	twenty-seven	sbet weshryn
سبعون	seventy	sabeun
ستة	six	st
ستة وعشرون	twenty-six	stt waeishrun
ستون	sixty	sutun
سجادة الحمام	bath mat	sajadat alhamam
سحب	pull	sahb
سطحية	shallow	satahia
سعيد	happy	saeid
سفينة	ship	safina
سقف	ceiling	saqf
سقف	roof	saqf
سكرتير	secretary	sikritir
سكين	knife	sikin
سلام	peace	salam
سلحفاة	turtle	silihafa
سم	poison	sm
سماء	sky	sama'
سمع	hear	sumie
سمك	fish	sammak
سميك	thick	samik
سن	tooth	sinn
سنتيمتر	centimeter	sanataymtr
سوق	market	suq
سيارة	car	sayara
سير	walk	sayr
سيئة	bad	sayiya
شاب	young	shabb

شاحنة	truck	shahina
شارع	street	sharie
شاشة	screen	shasha
شاطئ	beach	shati
شاي	tea	shay
شبكة	network	shabaka
شتاء	winter	shata'
شجرة	tree	shajara
شخص	person	shakhs
شرب	drinks	shurb
شرطة	police	shurta
شعر	hair	shaear
شفة	lip	shifa
شقة	apartment	shaqq
شقيق	brother	shaqiq
شمال	north	shamal
شمس	sun	shams
شهر	month	shahr
شهر اكتوبر	October	shahr 'uktubar
شوكة	fork	shawakk
صابون	soap	sabun
صالة عرض	gallery	salat earad
صباح	morning	sabah
صباح الخير	good morning	sabah alkhyr
صبي	boy	sabbi
صحافي	reporter	sahafi
صحي	healthy	sahi
صدر	chest	sadar
صغير	small	saghir
صفحة	page	safha
صفر	zero	sifr
صك	instrument	sak

صلة	relationship	sila
صلى	pray	salla
صندوق	box	sunduq
صهر	melt	sahr
صوت	sound	sawt
صوت	voice	sawt
صورة	image	sura
صورة	portrait	sura
ضحك	laugh	dahk
ضحية	victim	dahia
ضعيف	weak	daeif
ضفدع	frog	dafdae
ضمير	pronoun	damir
ضوء	light	daw'
ضيق	narrow	dayiq
ضيق	tight	dayiq
طاقة	energy	taqa
طالب علم	student	talab eilm
طائر	bird	tayir
طائرة	plane	tayira
طبخ	cook	tabbakh
طبق	plate	tabaq
طبيب	doctor	tabib
طبيعة	nature	tabiea
طريق	road	tariq
طعام	food	taeam
طعام	food	taeam
طعم	taste	taem
طفل	baby	tifl
طفل	child	tifl
طفل	child	tifl
طويل	long	tawil

Arabic	English	Transliteration
طويل	tall	tawil
طين	clay	tin
ظلام	dark	zalam
عال	loud	eal
عالي	high	eali
عام	year	eam
عد	count	eud
عرق	sweat	earaq
عشاء	dinner	easha'
عشب	grass	eshb
عشرة	ten	eshr
عشرون	twenty	eshrwn
عصير	juice	easir
عظم	bone	ezm
عقار	drug	eiqqar
عقد	contract	eaqad
علق	hang	ealaq
علم	science	eulim
علم	teach	eulim
على قيد الحياة	alive	ealaa qayd alhaya
عمدة	mayor	eumda
عمل	work	eamal
عميق	deep	eamiq
عين	eye	eayan
غابة	forest	ghaba
غبار	dust	ghabar
غداء	lunch	ghada'
غرب	west	gharb
غرفة	room	ghurfa
غرفة نوم	bedroom	ghurfat nawm
غسل	wash	ghasil
غنى	sing	ghina

غني	rich	ghani
غوريلا	gorilla	ghurila
فاتورة حساب	bill	fatturat hisab
فأر	mouse	fa'ar
فبراير	February	fibrayir
فتاة	girl	fatatan
فتاة	girl	fatatan
فتح	open	fath
فخذ	thigh	fakhudh
فراشة	butterfly	farashatan
فرقة	band	firqa
فستان	dress	fastan
فضفاض	loose	fadafad
فضي	silver	fadi
فقير	poor	faqir
فكر في	think	fakkar fi
فم	mouth	fam
فن	art	fan
فنان	artist	fannan
فوق	up	fawq
فوق	up	fawq
في الخارج	outside	fi alkharij
في داخل	inside	fi dakhil
في ذمة الله تعالى	dead	fi dhimmat alllah taealaa
فيل	elephant	fil
فيلم	movie	film
قارب	boat	qarib
قاموس	dictionary	qamus
قبض على	catch	qubid ealaa
قبعة	cap	qabea
قبعة	hat	qabea

قبلة	kiss	qibla
قبيح	ugly	qabih
قتل	kill	qutil
قتل	murder	qutil
قد	May	qad
قدم	foot	qadam
قديم	old	qadim
قذر	dirty	qadhar
قرب	near	qurb
قرد	monkey	qarrad
قصة	story	qiss
قصير	short	qasir
قط	cat	qat
قطار	train	qitar
قطع	cut	qate
قطعة	piece	qitea
قفازات	gloves	qafazat
قفز	jump	qafaz
قفل	lock	qafl
قلب	heart	qalb
قلم	pencil	qalam
قلم جاف	pen	qalam jaf
قميص	shirt	qamis
قهوة	coffee	qahuww
قوي	strong	qawi
قياس	measurements	qias
كانون الثاني	January	kanun alththani
كاهن	priest	kahin
كبير	big	kabir
كتاب	book	kitab
كتف	shoulder	kutuf
كحول	alcohol	kahul

عربي	English	transliteration
كرة	ball	kura
كرسي	chair	kursi
كريم	cream	karim
كنيسة	church	kanisa
كوب	cup	kub
كوع	elbow	kue
كيكة	cake	kayka
كيلوغرام	kilogram	kilughram
لا	no	la
لاعب	player	laeib
لحم بقري	beef	lahm baqari
لحم خنزير	pork	lahm khinzir
لحية	beard	lahia
لسان	tongue	lisan
لطيف	nice	latif
لعب	play	laeib
لعبة	game	lueba
لمس	touch	lams
لنا	our	lana
ليل	night	layl
ليمون	lemon	laymun
ماء	water	ma'an
مات	die	mat
مادة	material	madd
مارس	March	maris
مال	money	mal
مائة	one hundred	miaya
مباشرة	straight	mubashara
مبلل	wet	mublil
متجر	store	matjar
متر	meter	mitr
متفرقات	miscellaneous	mutafarriqat

مجلة	magazine	majall
محام	lawyer	muham
محرك	engine	maharrak
محرك	engine	maharrak
محطة	station	mahatt
محكمة	court	mahkama
محيط	ocean	mmuhit
مخيم	camp	mukhayam
مدرس	teacher	mudarris
مدرسة	school	madrasa
مدير	manager	mudir
مدينة	city	madina
مربع	square	murabbae
مرة	time	marr
مرحاض	toilet	mirhad
مرر	pass	marrar
مرشح	candidate	murashshah
مرض	disease	marad
مروحة	fan	muruha
مروحة	fan	muruha
مريض	sick	marid
مزج	mix	mizj
مزج	mix	mizj
مزرعة	farm	mazraea
مساء	evening	masa'
مستشفى	hospital	mustashfaa
مسرح	theater	masrah
مسطحة	flat	mustaha
مشروب كحولي	alcoholic drink	mashrub khuly
مصباح	lamp	misbah
مصعد	lift	museid
مطار	airport	matar

مطبخ	kitchen	mutbakh
مطر	rain	mtr
مطعم	restaurant	mateam
معدة	stomach	mueadd
معدن	metal	muedan
معطف	coat	muetaf
معطف	jacket	muetaf
مفتاح	key	miftah
مكالمة	call	mukalima
مكتب	office	maktab
مكتبة	library	maktaba
مكلفة	expensive	mukallafa
ملابس	clothing	malabis
ملاحظة	note	mulahaza
ملح	salt	milh
ملخص	abstract	mulakhkhas
ملعقة	spoon	maleaqa
ملك	king	malik
ملكة	queen	malika
مليار	billion	milyar
مليون	million	milyun
ممارسة	exercise	mumarasa
ممثلة	actress	mumaththila
منتزه	park	muntazzuh
منحن	curved	munhun
منخفض	low	munkhafid
منزل	house	manzil
منشفة	towel	tawl munshifat
منشفة الحمام	bath towel	alhamam
منعطف	turn	muneataf
موجة	wave	mawja

موز	banana	muz
موسمي	seasonal	mawsimi
موسيقى	music	musiqaa
موسيقي	musical	musiqi
موقع	location	mawqie
موقف	stand	mwqf
مؤلف	author	muallaf
مئة الف	one hundred thousand	miat 'alf
نادل	waiter	nadil
نار	fire	nar
ناعم	soft	naeam
نافذة	window	nafidha
نبات	plant	nabb'at
نجمة	star	najma
نحاس	copper	nahas
نحن	we	nahn
نسر	eagle	nusar
نصف	half	nsf
نظيف	clean	nazif
نعم فعلا	yes	nem fielaan
نفط	oil	nft
نقطة	dot	nuqta
نمط	pattern	namat
نهر	river	nahr
نوم	sleep	nawm
نووي	nuclear	nawawi
هاتف	phone	hatif
هاتف	telephone	hatif
هادئ	quiet	hadi
هجوم	Attack	hujum
هدية	Gift	hadia

هذا	it	hadha
هز	shake	hazz
هم	Them	hum
هم	They	hum
هو	he	hu
هواء	air	hawa'
هي	she	hi
واحد	one	wahid
واحد وعشرين	twenty-one	wahid weshryn
واسع	wide	wasie
واضح	clear	wadh
وجبة فطور	breakfast	wajubbat futur
وجه	face	wajjah
وردي	pink	waradi
ورقة	paper	waraqatan
ورقة الشجر	leaf	waraqat alshshajar
وزن	weight	wazn
وسائل النقل	transportation	wasayil alnnaql
وصمة	stain	wasamm
وظيفة	job	wazifa
وظيفة	Jobs	wazifa
ويسكي	whiskey	wayaski
يبيع	sell	yabie
يجري	run	yajri
يد	hand	yd
يرى	see	yaraa
يشترى	buy	yushtaraa
يشترى	buy	yushtaraa
يطير	fly	yatir
يقود	drive	yaqud
ينحني	bend	yanhani
يوليو	July	yuliu

يوم	Days	yawm
يوم السبت	Saturday	yawm alssabt
يوم غد	tomorrow	yawm ghad
يونيو	June	yuniu

Selected Verses From the Bible

For God so loved the world, that he gave his only begotten Son, that whosoever believeth in him should not perish, but have everlasting life. - John 3:16

For all have sinned, and come short of the glory of God; - Romans 3:23

For the wages of sin is death; but the gift of God is eternal life through Jesus Christ our Lord. - Romans 6:23

Jesus saith unto him, I am the way, the truth, and the life: no man cometh unto the Father, but by me. - John 14:6

And said, Verily I say unto you, Except ye be converted, and become as little children, ye shall not enter into the kingdom of heaven. - Matthew 18:3

And I give unto them eternal life; and they shall never perish, neither shall any man pluck them out of my hand. - John 10:28

But as many as received him, to them gave he power to become the sons of God, even to them that believe on his name: - John 1:12

Jesus answered and said unto him, Verily, verily, I say unto thee, Except a man be born again, he cannot see the kingdom of God. - John 3:3

He that believeth on the Son hath everlasting life: and he that believeth not the Son shall not see life; but the wrath of God abideth on him. - John 3:36

And they said, Believe on the Lord Jesus Christ, and thou shalt be saved, and thy house. - Acts 16:31

That if thou shalt confess with thy mouth the Lord Jesus, and shalt believe in thine heart that God hath raised him from the dead, thou shalt be saved. For with the heart man believeth unto righteousness; and with the mouth confession is made unto salvation. For whosoever shall call upon the name of the Lord shall be saved. - Romans 10:9,10,13

For by grace are ye saved through faith; and that not of yourselves: it is the gift of God: Not of works, lest any man should boast. - Ephesians 2:8,9

Not by works of righteousness which we have done, but according to his mercy he saved us, by the washing of regeneration, and renewing of the Holy Ghost; - Titus 3:5

And almost all things are by the law purged with blood; and without shedding of blood is no remission. - Hebrews 9:22

Therefore if any man be in Christ, he is a new creature: old things are passed away; behold, all things are become new. - II Corinthians 5:17

If we confess our sins, he is faithful and just to forgive us our sins, and to cleanse us from all unrighteousness. - I John 1:9

Behold, I stand at the door, and knock: if any man hear my voice, and open the door, I will come in to him, and will sup with him, and he with me. -

Revelation 3:20

آيات مختارة من الكتاب المقدس

لأَنَّهُ هَكَذَا أَحَبَّ اللهُ الْعَالَمَ حَتَّى بَذَلَ ابْنَهُ الْوَحِيدَ لِكَيْ لاَ يَهْلِكَ كُلُّ مَنْ يُؤْمِنُ بِهِ بَلْ تَكُونُ لَهُ الْحَيَاةُ الأَبَدِيَّةُ. - يوحنا 3: 16

إِذِ الْجَمِيعُ أَخْطَأُوا وَأَعْوَزَهُمْ مَجْدُ اللهِ - رومية 3: 23

لأَنَّ أُجْرَةَ الْخَطِيَّةِ هِيَ مَوْتٌ وَأَمَّا هِبَةُ اللهِ فَهِيَ حَيَاةٌ أَبَدِيَّةٌ بِالْمَسِيحِ يَسُوعَ رَبِّنَا. - رومية 6: 23

قَالَ لَهُ يَسُوعُ: «أَنَا هُوَ الطَّرِيقُ وَالْحَقُّ وَالْحَيَاةُ. لَيْسَ أَحَدٌ يَأْتِي إِلَى الآبِ إِلاَّ بِي. - يوحنا 14: 6

وَأَمَّا كُلُّ الَّذِينَ قَبِلُوهُ فَأَعْطَاهُمْ سُلْطَاناً أَنْ يَصِيرُوا أَوْلاَدَ اللهِ أَيِ الْمُؤْمِنُونَ بِاسْمِهِ. - يوحنا 1: 12

فَقَالَ يَسُوعُ: «الْحَقَّ الْحَقَّ أَقُولُ لَكَ: إِنْ كَانَ أَحَدٌ لاَ يُولَدُ مِنْ فَوْقُ لاَ يَقْدِرُ أَنْ يَرَى مَلَكُوتَ اللَّهِ». - يوحنا 3: 3

وَكُلُّ شَيْءٍ تَقْرِيباً يَتَطَهَّرُ حَسَبَ النَّامُوسِ بِالدَّمِ، وَبِدُونِ سَفْكِ دَمٍ لاَ تَحْصُلُ مَغْفِرَةٌ! - العبرانيين 9: 22

وَقَالَ: «اَلْحَقَّ أَقُولُ لَكُمْ: إِنْ لَمْ تَرْجِعُوا وَتَصِيرُوا مِثْلَ الأَوْلاَدِ فَلَنْ تَدْخُلُوا مَلَكُوتَ السَّمَاوَاتِ. ـ متى 18: 3

هَئَنَذَا وَاقِفٌ عَلَى الْبَابِ وَأَقْرَعُ. إِنْ سَمِعَ أَحَدٌ صَوْتِي وَفَتَحَ الْبَابَ، أَدْخُلُ إِلَيْهِ وَأَتَعَشَّى مَعَهُ وَهُوَ مَعِي. ـ رؤيا 3: 20

إِنِ اعْتَرَفْنَا بِخَطَايَانَا فَهُوَ أَمِينٌ وَعَادِلٌ، حَتَّى يَغْفِرَ لَنَا خَطَايَانَا وَيُطَهِّرَنَا مِنْ كُلِّ إِثْمٍ. ـ يوحنا 1: 9

لأَنَّكَ إِنِ اعْتَرَفْتَ بِفَمِكَ بِالرَّبِّ يَسُوعَ وَآمَنْتَ بِقَلْبِكَ أَنَّ اللهَ أَقَامَهُ مِنَ الأَمْوَاتِ خَلَصْتَ. لأَنَّ الْقَلْبَ يُؤْمَنُ بِهِ لِلْبِرِّ وَالْفَمَ يُعْتَرَفُ بِهِ لِلْخَلاَصِ. لأَنَّ كُلَّ مَنْ يَدْعُو بِاسْمِ الرَّبِّ يَخْلُصُ. ـ رومية 10: 9، 10، 13

لأَنَّكُمْ بِالنِّعْمَةِ مُخَلَّصُونَ، بِالإِيمَانِ، وَذَلِكَ لَيْسَ مِنْكُمْ. هُوَ عَطِيَّةُ اللهِ. لَيْسَ مِنْ أَعْمَالٍ كَيْلاَ يَفْتَخِرَ أَحَدٌ. ـ أفسس 2: 8، 9

لاَ بِأَعْمَالٍ فِي بِرٍّ عَمِلْنَاهَا نَحْنُ، بَلْ بِمُقْتَضَى رَحْمَتِهِ ـخَلَّصَنَا بِغَسْلِ الْمِيلاَدِ الثَّانِي وَتَجْدِيدِ الرُّوحِ الْقُدُسِ، ـ تيطس 3: 5

31فَقَالاَ: «آمِنْ بِالرَّبِّ يَسُوعَ الْمَسِيحِ فَتَخْلُصَ أَنْتَ وَأَهْلُ بَيْتِكَ». ـ أعمال الرسل 16: 31

اَلَّذِي يُؤْمِنُ بِالِابْنِ لَهُ حَيَاةٌ أَبَدِيَّةٌ وَالَّذِي لَا يُؤْمِنُ بِالِابْنِ لَنْ يَرَى حَيَاةً بَلْ

يَمْكُثُ عَلَيْهِ غَضَبُ اللَّهِ». ـ يوحنا 3: 36

وَأَنَا أُعْطِيهَا حَيَاةً أَبَدِيَّةً وَلَنْ تَهْلِكَ إِلَى الْأَبَدِ وَلَا يَخْطَفُهَا أَحَدٌ مِنْ يَدِي. ـ

يوحنا 10: 28

إِذاً إِنْ كَانَ أَحَدٌ فِي الْمَسِيحِ فَهُوَ خَلِيقَةٌ جَدِيدَةٌ. الْأَشْيَاءُ الْعَتِيقَةُ قَدْ مَضَتْ.

هُوَذَا الْكُلُّ قَدْ صَارَ جَدِيداً. ـ كورنثوس 5: 17

Sources Used

https://tsl620atnaz.wikispaces.com/Arabic?responseToken=8 35f88f4a83c239a926e6884f60c6342

https://en.wikipedia.org/wiki/Arabic

www.sonofgod.net

http://www.fodors.com/language/arabic

http://www.omniglot.com/writing/arabic.htm

http://learn101.org/arabic_nouns.php

http://www.effectivelanguagelearning.com/language-guide/arabic-language

http://www.myeasyarabic.com/site/what_is_spoken_arabic.htm

English translation of the Bible is from the King James Version.

The Arabic translation is Smith & Van Dyke version which is the most commonly used Arabic Bible.

Book Cover photo from

http://www.funonsite.com/wallpaper/islamic/13-rajab-jashan-imam-ali-pictures-6291.php

Used by permission

Made in the USA
Columbia, SC
23 July 2022

63906192R00104